U.S. ARMY ZOMBIE COMBAT SKILLS

U.S. ARMY ZOMBIE COMBAT SKILLS

DEPARTMENT OF THE ARMY

EDITED BY COLE LOUISON
ILLUSTRATIONS BY DAVID COLE WHEELER
UNDEAD COMBAT CONSULTANTS TO THE U.S. ARMY

LYONS PRESS
Guilford, Connecticut
An imprint of Globe Pequot Press

To buy books in quantity for corporate use
or incentives, call **(800) 962–0973**
or e-mail **premiums@GlobePequot.com**.

Lyons Press is an imprint of Globe Pequot Press.

Text designed by Libby Kingsbury

Library of Congress Cataloging-in-Publication Data is available on file.

ISBN 978-1-59921-909-7

Printed in the United States of America

10 9 8 7 6 5 4 3 2 1

CONTENTS

List of Illustrations ix

Introduction xiv

LIVING WARRIOR ETHOS 1

CHAPTER 1 THE WARRIOR 3
Operational Environment 3
Army Values 4
Living Law of Land Warfare 5
Warrior Culture 5
Battle Drill 6
Warrior Drills 6

CHAPTER 2 INDIVIDUAL READINESS 8
Predeployment 8
Legal Assistance 8
Personal Weapon 10

CHAPTER 3 ZOMBIE COMBAT CASUALTY CARE
AND PREVENTIVE MEDICINE 13
Section I. ZOMBIE COMBAT CASUALTY CARE 13
Combat Lifesaver 14
Lifesaving Measures (First Aid) 14
Casualty Evacuation 49
Section II. PREVENTIVE MEDICINE 59
Clothing and Sleeping Gear 60
Mental Health and Morale 61

CHAPTER 4 ENVIRONMENTAL CONDITIONS 63
Section I. DESERT 63
Types 64
Preparation 66
Section II. JUNGLE 70
Types 71
Preparation 74

Section III. ARCTIC   76
  Types   76
  Preparation   77

CHAPTER 5 COVER, CONCEALMENT, AND CAMOUFLAGE   79
Section I. COVER   79
  Natural Cover   80
  Man-Made Cover   80
Section II. CONCEALMENT   82
  Natural Concealment   83
  Actions as Concealment   83
Section III. CAMOUFLAGE   83
  Movement   84
  Positions   84
  Outlines and Shadows   84
  Shine   84
  Shape   85
  Colors   85
  Dispersion   85
  Preparation   87
  Individual Techniques   87

CHAPTER 6 FIGHTING POSITIONS   91
  Cover   91
  Concealment   93
  Camouflage   94
  Sectors and Fields of Fire   94
  Hasty and Deliberate Fighting Positions   96
  Two-Man Fighting Position   97
  One-Man Fighting Position   107
  Close Combat Missile Fighting Positions   112
  Range Cards   113

CHAPTER 7 MOVEMENT   128
  Individual Movement Techniques   128
  Immediate Actions While Moving   135
  Fire and Movement   136
  Movement on Vehicles   136

CHAPTER 8 URBAN AREAS 139
Section I. MOVEMENT TECHNIQUES 139
  Avoiding Open Areas 139
  Moving Parallel to Buildings 140
  Moving Past Windows 140
  Crossing a Wall 142
  Moving around Corners 142
  Moving within a Building 144
Section II. OTHER PROCEDURES 145
  Entering a Building 145
  Clearing a Room 151
Section III. FIGHTING POSITIONS 154
  Hasty Fighting Position 154
  Prepared Fighting Position 158

CHAPTER 9 "EVERY SOLDIER IS A SENSOR" 162
  Definition 162
  Resources 163
  Forms of Questioning 165
  Report Levels 166
  SALUTE Format 167
  Handling and Reporting of the Undead 167
  Operations Security 170
  Observation Techniques 171
  Limited Visibility Observation 173
  Range Estimation 179

CHAPTER 10 COMBAT MARKSMANSHIP 182
  Safety 182
  Administrative Procedures 183
  Weapons 184
  Fire Control 194
  Combat Zero 198
  Shot Groups 198
  Misfire Procedures and Immediate Action 199
  Reflexive Fire 202

CHAPTER 11 COMMUNICATIONS 207
Section I. MEANS OF COMMUNICATION 207
 Messengers 207
 Wire 208
 Visual Signals 208
 Sound 210
 Radio 210
Section II. RADIOTELEPHONE PROCEDURES 211
 Rules 211
 Types of Nets 212
 Precedence of Reports 212
 Message Format 212
 Common Messages 213
 Prowords 214
 Operation on a Net 216
Section III. COMMUNICATIONS SECURITY 216
 Classifications 217
 Signal Operating Instructions 217
 Automated Net Control Device 218
Section IV. EQUIPMENT 220
 Radios 220
 Wire 222
 Telephone Equipment 223

CHAPTER 12 SURVIVAL, EVASION, RESISTANCE, AND ESCAPE 224
 Survival 224
 Evasion 227
 Resistance 231
 Escape 234
 Concealment 235

 Glossary 236

LIST OF ILLUSTRATIONS

Figure   Page

1-1   Army Values   4
1-2   Warrior Drills   7
2-1   Example personal predeployment checklist   9
3-1   Assessment   18
3-2   Airway blocked by tongue   19
3-3   Airway opened by extending neck   20
3-4   Jaw thrust technique   20
3-5   Head-tilt/chin-lift technique   21
3-6   Checking for breathing   22
3-7   Rescue breathing   23
3-8   Placement of fingers to detect pulse   25
3-9   Abdominal thrust on unresponsive casualty   27
3-10   Hand placement for chest thrust   28
3-11   Breastbone depresses 1½ to 2 inches   29
3-12   Opening of casualty's mouth, tongue-jaw lift   30
3-13   Opening of casualty's mouth, crossed-finger method   30
3-14   Use of finger to dislodge a foreign body   30
3-15   Emergency bandage   32
3-16   Application of pad to wound   33
3-17   Insertion of bandage into pressure bar   33
3-18   Tightening of bandage   33
3-19   Pressure of bar into bandage   33
3-20   Wrapping of bandage over pressure bar   33
3-21   Securing of bandage   33
3-22   Grasping of dressing tails with both hands   34
3-23   Pulling dressing open   34
3-24   Placement of dressing directly on wound   35
3-25   Wrapping of dressing tail around injured part   35
3-26   Tails tied into nonslip knot   35
3-27   Application of direct manual pressure   36
3-28   Elevation of injured limb   36
3-29   Wad of padding on top of field dressing   37

3-30	Improvised dressing over wad of padding	37
3-31	Ends of improvised dressing wrapped tightly around limb	37
3-32	Ends of improvised dressing tied together in nonslip knot	38
3-33	Digital pressure (fingers, thumbs, or hands)	39
3-34	Zombie application tourniquet	41
3-35	Improved zombie first aid kit	42
3-36	Tourniquet above knee	43
3-37	Rigid object on top of half knot	44
3-38	Tourniquet knotted over rigid object and twisted	45
3-39	Free ends tied on side of limb	45
3-40	Fireman's carry	51–52
3-41	Alternate fireman's carry	53
3-42	Supporting carry	54
3-43	Neck drag	54
3-44	Cradle-drop drag	55
3-45	Two-man support carry	56
3-46	Two-man fore-and-aft carry	57
3-47	Two-hand seat carry	57
3-48	Rules for avoiding illness in the field	59
3-49	Care of the feet	60
5-1	Natural cover	79
5-2	Cover along a wall	80
5-3	Man-made cover	80
5-4	Body armor and helmet	81
5-5	Protective cover against chemical/biological warfare agents	82
5-6	Concealment	82
5-7	Soldier in arctic camouflage	86
5-8	Camouflage soldiers	86
5-9	Camouflaged helmet	87
5-10	Advanced camouflage face paint	89
6-1	Man-made cover	92
6-2	Cover	93
6-3	Prone position (hasty)	97
6-4	Establishment of sectors and building method	99

6-5	Two-man fighting position (Stage 1)	100
6-6	Placement of OHC supports and construction of retaining walls	100
6-7	Two-man fighting position (Stage 2)	101
6-8	Digging of position (side view)	102
6-9	Placement of stringers for OHC (Stage 3)	102
6-10	Two-man fighting position	103
6-11	Revetment construction	103
6-12	Grenade sumps	104
6-13	Storage compartments	104
6-14	Installation of overhead cover	106
6-15	Two-man fighting position with built-up OHC (Stage 4)	106
6-16	Two-man fighting position with built-down OHC (top view)	108
6-17	Two-man fighting position with built-down OHC (side view)	108
6-18	Position with firing platforms	110
6-19	Grenade sump locations	111
6-20	Machine gun fighting position with OHC	112
6-21	Standard Javelin fighting position	114
6-22	Primary sector with an FPL	117
6-23	Complete sketch with PDF	118
6-24	Data section	118
6-25	Example completed data section	120
6-26	Example completed range card	122
6-27	Reference points and target reference points	123
6-28	Maximum engagement lines	125
6-29	Weapon reference point	126
7-1	Low and high crawl	130
7-2	Rush	131
7-3	Fire team wedge	134
7-4	Following of team leader from impact area	135
7-5	Mounting and riding arrangements	138
8-1	Soldier moving past windows	141
8-2	Soldier passing basement windows	141
8-3	Soldier crossing a wall	142

8-4	Correct technique for looking around a corner	143
8-5	*Pie-ing* a corner	143
8-6	Movement within a building	144
8-7	Lower-level entry technique with support bar	147
8-8	Lower-level entry technique without support bar	147
8-9	Lower-level entry two-man pull technique	147
8-10	Lower-level entry one-man lift technique	148
8-11	Some considerations for selecting and occupying individual fighting positions	155
8-12	Soldier firing left or right handed	156
8-13	Soldier firing around a corner	156
8-14	Soldier firing from peak of a roof	157
8-15	Emplacement of machine gun in a doorway	160
9-1	Potential indicators	164
9-2	Rapid/slow-scan pattern	172
9-3	Detailed search	173
9-4	Typical scanning pattern	174
9-5	Off-center viewing	175
9-6	AN/PVS-7 and AN/PVS-14	176
9-7	AN/PAS-13, V1, V2, and V3	177
9-8	AN/PAQ-4 series and the AN/PEQ-2A	178
9-9	Mil-relation formula	181
10-1	M9 pistol	185
10-2	M16A2 rifle	186
10-3	M4 carbine	187
10-4	M203 grenade launcher	187
10-5	M249 squad automatic weapon (SAW)	188
10-6	M240B machine gun	189
10-7	M2 .50 caliber machine gun with M3 tripod mount	190
10-8	MK 19 grenade machine gun, Mod 3	191
10-9	Improved M72 LAW	192
10-10	M136 AT4	193
10-11	M141 BDM	194
10-12	Javelin	195
10-13	Final shot group results	199
10-14	Ready positions	204
11-1	Common prowords	215

11-2	Automated net control device	218
11-3	Automated net control device keypad	219
11-4	Call signs	220
11-5	AN/PRC-148 multiband intrateam radio (MBITR)	221
11-6	IC-F43 portable UHF transceiver	222
11-7	AN/PRC-119A-D SIP	222
12-1	SURVIVAL	225
12-2	Tool for remembering shelter locations	228
12-3	Code of Conduct	232

INTRODUCTION

Combat with the Undead is chaotic, intense, and shockingly destructive. In your first battle, you will experience the confusing and often terrifying sights, sounds, smells, and dangers of the zombie battlefield—but you must learn to survive and win despite them.

1. You could face a fierce and relentless Undead enemy.
2. You could be surrounded by destruction, death, and reanimated corpses.
3. Your leaders may shout urgent commands, lost in the drone of the advancing Undead enemy.
4. Friendly fire rounds might impact near you.
5. The air could be filled with the smell of explosives, propellant, and decaying flesh.
6. You might hear the screams of a devoured comrade.

However, even in all this confusion and fear, remember that you are not alone. You are part of a well-trained team, backed by the most powerful combined arms force, and the most modern technology in the world. You must keep faith with your fellow Soldiers, remember your training, and do your duty to the best of your ability. Also remember that the enemy has no faith, no training, and only the crudest weaponry. If you do, and you uphold your Warrior Ethos, you can win and return home with honor.

This is the Soldier's Zombie Combat FM. It tells the Soldier how to perform the combat skills needed to survive on the battlefield against the Undead. All Soldiers, across all branches and components, must learn these basic skills. Noncommissioned officers (NCOs) must ensure that their Soldiers receive training on—and know—these vital combat skills.

LIVING
WARRIOR
ETHOS

What is the Living Warrior Ethos? At first glance, it is just four simple lines embedded in the Living Warrior's Creed. Yet, it is the spirit represented by these four lines that:

- Compels Warriors to fight through all adversity, under any circumstances, in order to achieve victory.

- Represents the Living Warrior's loyal, tireless, and selfless commitment to his nation, his mission, his unit, his Living race, and his fellow Warriors.

- Captures the essence of combat, Army Values, and Warrior Culture.

Sustained and developed through discipline, commitment, and pride, these four lines motivate every Warrior to persevere and, ultimately, to refuse defeat. These lines go beyond mere survival. They speak to forging life over death, victory from chaos; to overcoming fear, hunger, deprivation, and fatigue; and to accomplishing the mission:

THE WARRIOR'S CREED

I am a Living American Soldier.

I am a fighter and a member of a team.

I serve the Living people of the United States and live the Army Values.

I will always place the mission first.

I will never accept defeat.

I will never quit.

I will never leave a fallen comrade.

I will not hesitate to terminate comrades bitten by the Undead.

I am disciplined, physically and mentally tough, trained and proficient in my Warrior tasks and drills.

I always maintain my arms, my equipment, and myself.

I am an expert and I am a professional.

I stand ready to deploy, engage, and destroy the Undead enemies of the United States of America in close combat.

I am a guardian of freedom and the American way of life.

I am a Living American Soldier.

CHAPTER 1

THE WARRIOR

Military service is more than a "job." It is a profession with the enduring purpose to win wars and destroy the Undead during a zombie uprising. The Living Warrior Ethos demands a dedication to duty that may involve putting your life on the line, even when survival is in question, for a cause greater than yourself. As a Soldier, you must motivate yourself to rise above the worst battle conditions—no matter what it takes, or how long it takes. That is the heart of the Warrior Ethos, which is the foundation for your commitment to victory in times of peace and war. While always exemplifying the four parts of Warrior Ethos, you must have absolute faith in yourself and your team, as they are trained and equipped to destroy the Undead in close combat. Warrior drills are a set of nine battle drills, consisting of individual tasks that develop and manifest the Warrior Ethos in Soldiers.

OPERATIONAL ENVIRONMENT

1-1. This complex operational environment offers no relief or rest from contact with the Undead across the spectrum of conflict. No matter what combat conditions you find yourself in, you must turn your personal Warrior Ethos into your commitment to win. In the combat environment of today, unlike conflicts of the past, there is little distinction between the forward and rear areas. Battlefields of the Global War on Zombie-ism, and battles to be fought in the US Army's future, are and will be frightening, asymmetrical, violent, unpredictable, and multidimensional. Today's conflicts are fought throughout the whole spectrum of the battlespace by all Soldiers, regardless of military occupational specialty (MOS). Every

Soldier must be ready and able to enter combat; ready to fight—and win—against the Undead, *any* time, *any* place.

ARMY VALUES

1-2. US Army Values reminds us and displays to the rest of the Living world—the civilian governments we serve, the nation we protect, other nations, and even the Undead—who we are and what we stand for (Figure 1-1). The trust you have for your fellow Soldiers, and the trust the Living people have in you, depends on how well you live up to the Army Values. After all, these values are the fundamental building blocks that enable you to understand right from wrong in any situation. Army Values are consistent and support one another; you cannot follow one value and ignore the others. Figure 1-1 shows the Army Values, which form the acrostic LDRSHIP.

Loyalty	Bear true faith and allegiance to the Constitution, the Army, your unit, and other Soldiers.
Duty	Fulfill your obligations.
Respect	Treat people with dignity as they should be treated.
Selfless Service	Put the welfare of the nation, the Army, and your subordinates before your own.
Honor	Live up to all the Army Values.
Integrity	Do what's right, legally and morally.
Personal Courage (Physical or Moral)	Face fear, danger, or adversity.

Figure 1-1. Army Values.

1-3. Performance in combat, the greatest challenge, requires a basis, such as Army Values, for motivation and will. In these values are rooted the basis for the character and self-discipline that generates the will to succeed and the motivation to persevere. From this motivation derived through tough realistic training and the skills acquired, which will make you successful, a Soldier who "walks the walk."

1-4. Army Values, including policies and procedures, form the foundation on which the Army's institutional culture stands. However, written values are useless unless practiced. You must act correctly with character, complete understanding, and sound motivation. Your trusted leaders will aid you in adopting such values by making sure their core experiences validate them. By this method, strategic leadership embues Army Values into all Soldiers.

LIVING LAW OF LAND WARFARE

1-5. The conduct of armed hostilities on land is regulated by FM 27-10 and the Living Law of Land Warfare. Their purpose is to diminish the evils of war by protecting combatants *and* noncombatants from unnecessary suffering, and by safeguarding certain fundamental Living human rights of those who fall into the hands of the Undead, particularly Undead prisoners of war (UPWs), detainees, wounded and sick, and civilians. Every Soldier adheres to these laws, and ensures that his subordinates adhere to them as well, during the conduct of their duties. Soldiers must also seek clarification from their superiors of any unclear or apparently illegal order. Soldiers need to understand that the law of land warfare not only applies to states, but also to individuals, particularly all members of the armed forces.

WARRIOR CULTURE

1-6. The Warrior Culture, a shared set of important beliefs, values, and assumptions, is crucial and perishable. Therefore, the Army must continually affirm, develop, and sustain it, as it maintains the nation's existence. Its martial ethic connects American warriors of today with those whose previous sacrifices allowed our nation to persevere. You, the individual Soldier, are the foundation for this Culture. As in larger institutions, the Armed Forces' use culture, in this case Warrior Culture, to let people know they are part of something bigger than just themselves; they have responsibilities not only to the people around them, but also to those who have gone before and to those who will come after them. The Warrior Culture is a part of who you are, and a custom you can take pride in. Personal courage, loyalty to comrades, and dedication to duty are attributes integral to putting your life up against the Undead.

BATTLE DRILL

1-7. A battle drill—

- Is a collective action, executed by a platoon or smaller element, without the application of a deliberate decision-making process. The action is vital to success in combat or critical to preserve life. The drill is initiated on a cue, such as Undead action or your leader's order, and is a trained response to that stimulus. It requires minimum leader orders to accomplish, and is standard throughout the Army. A drill has the following advantages:

  - It is based on unit missions and the specific tasks, standards, and performance measures required to support mission proficiency.
  - It builds from simple to complex, but focuses on the basics.
  - It links how-to-train and how-to-fight at small-unit levels.
  - It provides an agenda for continuous coaching and analyzing.
  - It develops leaders, and builds teamwork and cohesion under stress.
  - It enhances the chance for individual and unit survival on the battlefield.

WARRIOR DRILLS

1-8. The Warrior drills—

- Are a set of core battle drills for small units from active and reserve component organizations across the Army, regardless of branch.
- Describe a training method for small units. This method requires training individual, leader, and collective tasks before the conduct of critical wartime missions.
- Provide a foundation for the development of specific objectives for combat. The expanded list of Warrior Drills helps place the individual Soldiers' tasks (as well as the team) in sufficient context to identify meaningful consequences of individual behavior.

- Have individual tasks that develop and manifest the Warrior Ethos. A *barrier*, for example, is an element that impedes a response or behavior. *Barrier control* can focus on points that are most sensitive to the behavior of individuals such as choices, actions, and interactions; and on those with the most serious consequences such as effects on other individuals and success of the mission.
- Create opportunities to develop the Warrior Ethos. The nine drills follow:

---

1. React to Contact (Visual, auditory, Direct Bombardment)

2. React to Slow Charge (Near)

3. React to Slow Charge (Far)

4. React to Indirect Bombardment

5. React to Attack of the Radioactive Undead

6. Break Contact

7. Dismount a Vehicle

8. Evacuate Mauled or Infected Personnel from Vehicle

9. Secure at a Halt

Figure 1-2. Warrior drills.

CHAPTER 2

INDIVIDUAL READINESS

The US Army is based on our nation's greatest resource—you, the individual fighting Soldier. Success in the defense of the Living race depends on your individual readiness, initiative, and capabilities. You are cohesive, integral parts of the whole. Your mission is to deter aggression through combat readiness and, when deterrence fails, to win the Living's wars. This mission must not be compromised. You must be ready.

Deployment is challenging and stressful—both on you and on your family. You will be away from the comforts of home. This is not easy. Preparedness can reduce the stress and increase your focus and confidence once you are deployed.

PREDEPLOYMENT

2-1. What could or would happen if you were a long way from your family for an indefinite period of time, and unable to communicate with them? The losing organization will complete a DA Form 7425, *Readiness and Deployment Checklist*, on you, but it is not designed for your use. Figure 2-1 shows an example checklist that you might create for your own use.

LEGAL ASSISTANCE

2-2. Your Living legal assistance center can provide a great number of services. Living legal assistance centers provide answers and advice to even the most complex problems. Such legal assistance usually does not include in-court representation. Some of the issues that your installation's legal assistance center may be able to help with follow:

Defense Enrollment Eligibilty Reporting System (DEERS)	Verify your DEERS information and ensure your family members can get needed medical care in your absence.
Dental Records	Update if needed.
Documents, Locations of	Ensure that your spouse or other family member(s) know where to find all of the above documents.
DD Form 93 Emergency Data Record	Check to ensure this is current and correct.
Eyeglasses and Protective Mask Inserts	Ensure you have two pairs of eyeglasses and protective mask inserts, all with your current prescription, if required.
Family Assistance Army Community Service (ACS)	Tell your family where to get various kinds of support and help while you are gone.
Legal Aid, Military	Tell your spouse where to get military legal aid in your absence.
Readiness Group (FRG)	Tell your family where to get various kinds of support and help while you are gone.
Finances	Ensure your spouse has access to all of your records and accounts and update them as needed.
Identification	Ensure you have two sets of these, if required.
Legal	See Family Assistance.
Life Insurance	Designate your beneficiary on SGLV Forms 8286 and 8286A, Soldier's Group Life Insurance (SGLI) Election and Certificate.
Directive, Advance	Specify any decisions you wish others to make on your behalf should you be unable to do so for yourself.
Medical (see also Power of Attorney) DD Form 2766 (Shot Record)	Keep your vaccinations and immunizations current.
Directive, Advance	Prepare if you want to specify how decisions are made on your behalf should you be unable to do so for yourself.
Living Will	Prepare if desired.
Records	Update if needed.
Warnings Tags	Ensure you have two sets of these, if required.
Power of Attorney General	Prepare to allow someone to perform all duties for you in your absence.
Medical, Durable	Prepare one of these to designate who makes decisions for you or your dependents, including your minor children, should a medical emergency occur while you are deployed or otherwise unable to make the decision yourself.
Special	Prepare to allow someone to perform a particular kind of duty for you in your absence.
Property	Prepare or update accounts, documents, and records as needed.
Service Record	Check to ensure this is current and correct.
Training	Update your weapon qualification(s), if needed.
Will(s)	Prepare new or update existing, for you and your spouse, if needed.

Figure 2-1. Example personal predeployment checklist.

- Marriage and divorce issues.
- Child custody and visitation issues.
- Adoptions or other family matters (as expertise is available).
- Wills.
- Powers of attorney.
- Advice for designating SGLI (Soldier's Group Life Insurance) beneficiaries.
- Landlord-tenant issues.

- Consumer affairs such as mortgages, warranties.
- Bankruptcies.
- Garnishments and indebtedness.
- Notarizations.
- Name changes, as expertise is available.
- Bars to reenlistment (as available).
- Hardship discharges.
- Taxes.

PERSONAL WEAPON

2-3. Your personal weapon is vital to you in combat. Take care of it, and it will do the same for you. Seems obvious, right? Apparently not. Multiple reports from the opening days of Operation Transylvanian Freedom revealed that faulty weapons training and maintenance were the main causes of Living casualties and captures: "These malfunctions may have resulted from inadequate individual maintenance and the environment." Soldiers had trouble firing their personal and crew-served weapons, and the main reason cited was poor preventive maintenance. Few things will end a firefight faster and more badly than a weapon that will not shoot! The complex M16A2 rifle needs cleaning and proper lubrication at least once a day in order to properly function. Follow these procedures and those in the technical manual (TM):

CLEANING

2-4. Use only the cleaning supplies listed in the *Expendable and Durable Items List* in the back of the TM.

Abrasives and Harsh Chemicals

2-5. Avoid using abrasive materials such as steel wool or commercial scrubbing pads, and harsh chemicals not intended for use on your weapon. This can ruin the finish of the weapon. It can also remove rifling and damage internal parts, either of which can make your weapon inaccurate and ineffective during the mission.

Water

2-6. Never clean your weapon under running water, which can force moisture into tight places, resulting in corrosion.

Frequency

2-7. In the field, clean your weapon often, at least daily. Even just taking every chance to wipe the weapon's exterior with a clean cloth will help ensure operability.

Disassembly

2-8. Do any cleaning that involves disassembly at your level in an enclosed area. Blowing sand and other debris can not only affect your weapon, it can also cause you to lose the parts of the weapon. For parts that must be disassembled beyond your level, such as the trigger assembly, just blow out the dirt or debris.

Magazines and Ammunition

2-9. Clean your magazines, but avoid using any lubrication in them or on ammunition. Unload and wipe off your ammunition daily, then disassemble and run a rag through the magazine to prevent jamming.

LUBRICATING

2-10. Lubrication reduces friction between metal parts.

Lubricant

2-11. You may only use authorized, standard military lubricant for small arms such as cleaner lubricant preservative (CLP). Also, lubricate only internal parts.

Moving Parts

2-12. Pay special attention to moving parts like the bolt carrier. Wipe the outside of the weapon dry.

Covers and Caps

2-13. Use rifle covers and muzzle caps to keep blowing debris and dust out of the muzzle and ejection port area. Cover mounted machine guns when possible. Keep your rifle's ejection port cover closed and a magazine inserted.

Humid Environments

2-14. Keep in mind that, in more humid environments such as jungles and swamps, you will need to use more lubrication, more often, on all metal parts. Temperature and other extreme weather conditions also factor in.

Desert Environments

2-15. Corrosion poses little threat in the desert. Avoid using too much lubrication, because it attracts sand.

Note: Maintain all issued equipment and clothing based on the specific care and maintenance instructions provided.

CHAPTER 3

ZOMBIE COMBAT CASUALTY CARE AND PREVENTIVE MEDICINE

Combat casualty care is the treatment administered to a wounded Soldier after he has been moved out of an engagement area or the Undead have been suppressed. This level of care can help save life and limb until medical personnel arrive. Soldiers might have to depend upon their own first-aid knowledge and skills to save themselves (self-aid) or another Soldier (buddy aid or combat lifesaver skills). This knowledge and training can possibly save a life, prevent permanent disability, or reduce long periods of hospitalization. The only requirement is to know what to do—and what not to do—in certain instances.

Personal hygiene and preventive medicine are simple, common-sense measures that each Soldier can perform to protect his health and that of others. Taking these measures can greatly reduce time lost due to disease and nonbattle injury.

SECTION 1. ZOMBIE COMBAT CASUALTY CARE

The Army warfighter doctrine, developed for a widely dispersed and rapidly moving battlefield, recognizes that battlefield constraints limit the number of trained medical personnel available to provide immediate, far-forward care. This section defines combat lifesaver, provides life-saving measures (first aid) techniques, and discusses casualty evacuation.

COMBAT LIFESAVER

3-1. The role of the combat lifesaver was developed to increase far-forward care to battle. At least one member—though ideally *every* member of each squad, team, and crew—should be a trained combat lifesaver. The leader is seldom a combat lifesaver, since he will have less time to perform those duties than would another member of his unit.

3-2. So what exactly is a combat lifesaver? He is a nonmedical combat Soldier. His *secondary* mission is to help the combat medic provide basic emergency care to bitten or mauled members of his squad, team, or crew, and to aid in evacuating them, mission permitting. He complements, rather than replaces, the combat medic. He receives training in enhanced first aid and selected medical procedures such as initiating intravenous uninfected blood infusions. Combat lifesaver training bridges the first aid training (self-aid or buddy aid, or SABA) given to all Soldiers in basic training, and the more advanced medical training given to Medical Specialists (MOS 91W), also known as combat medics.

3-3. The Living Academy of Health Sciences developed the Combat Lifesaver Course as part of its continuing effort to provide health service support to the Army. The current edition of the Combat Lifesaver Course lasts three days. The first day tests the buddy-aid tasks, and the other two days teach and test specific medical tasks.

LIFESAVING MEASURES (FIRST AID)

3-4. When a Soldier is bitten, scratched, or mauled, he must receive first aid immediately. Most injured or ill Soldiers can return to their units to fight or support. This is mainly, because they receive appropriate and timely first aid, followed by the best possible medical care. To help ensure this happens, every Soldier should have combat lifesaver training on basic lifesaving procedures (Table 3-1).

CHECK FOR BREATHING
3-5. Check first to see if the casualty's heart is beating, then to see if he is breathing. This paragraph discusses what to do in each possible situation.

1	Check for BREATHING	Lack of oxygen, due either to compromised airway or inadequate breathing, can cause brain damage or, when accompanied by zombie infection, Undeath in just a few minutes. Also be wary of droning or extremely foul breath. Both are early signs of Undeath that if detected require you to restrain or terminate the victim.
2	Check for BLEEDING vs OOZING	Life can continue only with sufficient blood to carry oxygen to tissues. Blood pumped through a Living body can escape at an alarming rate when the victim is wounded. When dressing a wound, however (see section 3-27), pay close attention: if the wound begins to ooze instead of bleed, or if the area around the wound begins to bubble and spread, these are signs of zombie-ism and you must act accordingly, either applying a tourniquet or terminating the victim.
3	Check for SHOCK	Unless shock is prevented, first aid performed, and medical treatment provided, Undeath may result in an infected victim, even with an otherwise nonfatal injury. Note that the first signs of shock are also the first signs of zombie-ism: slow reflexes, drool, glazed or hollow eyes, low body temp, clammy skin, and thus it can be hard to decipher between shock and early Undeath. Proceed with caution.

Table 3-1. First Aid.

React to Stoppage of Heartbeat

3-6. If a casualty's heart stops beating, you must both immediately seek medical help and be prepared to fight or terminate your infected comrade. The window between dead and Undead closes fast. You must move quickly in this gap of time to save your fellow Soldier—for if you can't save him he will become Undead and require termination. Thus, *seconds count!* Stoppage of the heart is soon followed by cessation of respiration, unless that has already happened. Remain calm, but think first, and act quickly. When a casualty's heart stops, he has no pulse. He is unconscious and limp, and his pupils are open wide. When evaluating a casualty, or when performing the preliminary steps of rescue breathing, feel for a pulse. If you *do not* detect a pulse, seek medical help.

Open Airway and Restore Breathing

3-7. All humans need oxygen to live. Oxygen breathed into the lungs gets into the bloodstream. The heart pumps the blood, which carries the oxygen throughout the body to the cells, which require a constant supply of oxygen. Without a constant supply of oxygen to the cells in the brain, we can suffer permanent brain damage, paralysis, or become Undead.

Assess and Position Casualty

3-8. To assess the casualty, do the following:

1. *Check* for responsiveness (A, Figure 3-1). Establish whether the casualty is conscious by gently shaking him and asking, "Are you OK?"
2. *Call* for help, if appropriate (B, Figure 3-1).
3. *Position* the unconscious casualty so that he is lying on his back and on a firm surface (C, Figure 3-1).

WARNING

If the casualty is lying on his chest (prone), cautiously roll him as a unit, so that his body does not twist. Twisting him could complicate a back, neck, or spinal injury.

4. Straighten his legs. Take the arm nearest to you, and move it so that it is straight and above his head. Repeat for the other arm.

5. Kneel beside the casualty with your knees near his shoulders. Leave room to roll his body (B, Figure 3-1). Place one hand behind his head and neck for support. With your other hand, grasp him under his far arm (C, Figure 3-1).

6. Roll him towards you with a steady, even pull. Keep his head and neck in line with his back.

7. Return his arms to his side. Straighten his legs, and reposition yourself so that you are kneeling at the level of his shoulders.

8. If you suspect a neck injury, and you are planning to use the jaw-thrust technique, then kneel at the casualty's head while looking toward his feet.

Open Airway of Unconscious or Nonbreathing Casualty

3-9. The tongue is the single most common airway obstruction (Figure 3-2). In most cases, just using the head-tilt/chin-lift technique can clear the airway. This pulls the tongue away from the air passage (Figure 3-3).

3-10. Call for help, and then position the casualty. Move (roll) him onto his back (C, Figure 3-1). Perform a finger sweep. If you see foreign material or vomit in the casualty's mouth, promptly remove it, but avoid spending much time doing so. Open the airway using the jaw-thrust or head-tilt/chin-lift technique.

Perform Jaw-Thrust Technique

3-11. Place your hands on both sides of the angles of the casualty's lower jaw, and lift with both hands. Displace the jaw forward and up (Figure 3-4). Your elbows should rest on the surface where the casualty is lying. If his lips close, you can use your thumb to retract his lower lip. If you have to give mouth-to-mouth, then close his nostrils by placing your cheek tightly against them. Carefully support his head without tilting it backward or turning it from side to side. This technique is the safest, and thus the first, to use to open the airway of a casualty who has a suspected

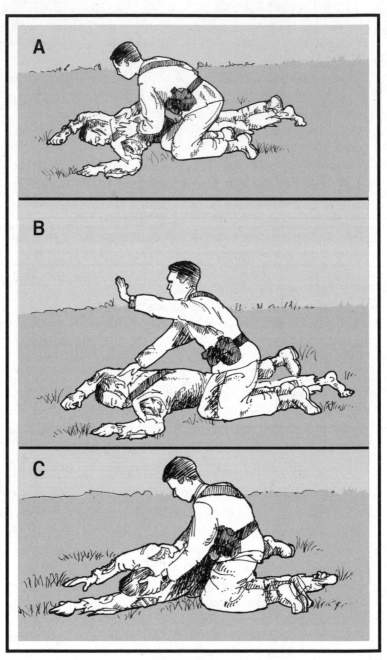

Figure 3-1. Assessment.

neck injury. Why? Because, you can usually do it *without* extending his neck. However, if you are having a hard time keeping his head from moving, you might have to try tilting his head back *very* slightly.

CAUTION

Although the head-tilt/chin-lift technique is an important procedure in opening the airway, take extreme care with it, because while you are trying to save a comrade, it may already be too late and thus you are in close quarters with a zombie. Proceed with caution. Watch for yellowing of the teeth, dilated eyes, peeling or bubbling skin. If you note any of these symptoms, cease all contact with the wounded's mouth. Furthermore, using too much force while performing this maneuver can cause more spinal injury. In a casualty with a suspected neck injury or severe head trauma, the safest approach to opening the airway is the jaw-thrust technique because, in most cases, you can do it without extending the casualty's neck.

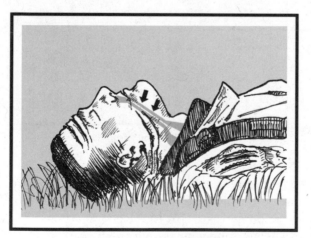

Figure 3-2. Airway blocked by tongue.

Figure 3-3. Airway opened by extending neck.

Figure 3-4. Jaw thrust technique.

Perform Head-Tilt/Chin-Lift Technique

3-12. Place one palm on the casualty's forehead and apply firm, backward pressure to tilt his head back. Place the fingertips of your other hand under the bony part of his lower jaw, and then lift, bringing his chin forward. Avoid using your thumb to lift his chin. Keep a close eye on the casualty's incisors. (Figure 3-5).

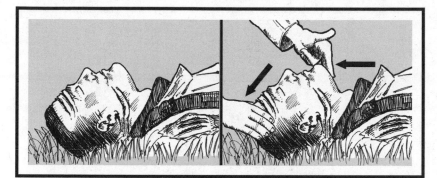
Figure 3-5. Head-tilt/chin-lift technique.

WARNING

Avoid pressing too deeply into the soft tissue under the casualty's chin, because you might obstruct his airway.

Check for Breathing while Maintaining Airway

3-13.
1. *Look* for his chest to rise and fall. Watch for unusual amounts of drool.
2. *Listen* for sound of breathing by placing your ear near his mouth. Listen close: moaning is an early sign of zombie-ism.
3. *Feel* for the flow of air on your cheek. Breath should be clean, clear, fresh. Bad breath is a bad sign.
4. *Perform* rescue breathing if he fails to resume breathing spontaneously and there are no signs of zombie-ism.

Note: *If the casualty resumes breathing, monitor and maintain the open airway. Ensure he is transported to a lockdown medical treatment facility as soon as possible. Although the casualty might be trying to breathe, his airway might still be obstructed. If so, open his airway (remove the obstruction) and keep the airway open (maintain his airway).*

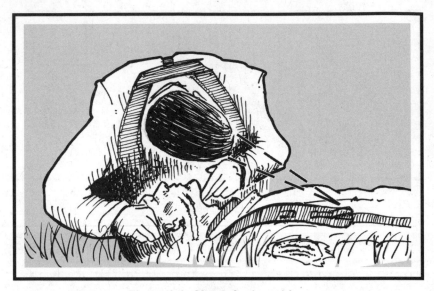
Figure 3-6. Checking for breathing.

Perform Rescue Breathing or Artificial Respiration

3-14. If the casualty fails to promptly resume adequate spontaneous breathing after the airway is open, you must start rescue breathing (artificial respiration, or mouth-to-mouth). Remain calm and armed, but think and act quickly. The sooner you start rescue breathing, the more likely you are to restore his breathing. If you are not sure if the casualty is breathing, give him artificial respiration anyway. It cannot hurt him. If he is breathing, you can see and feel his chest move and, if you put your hand or ear close to his mouth and nose, you can hear him expelling air. The preferred method of rescue breathing is mouth-to-mouth, but you cannot always use it. For example, if the casualty has a severe jaw fracture or mouth wound, extended incisors, or if his lips are bubbling, peeling, or suppurating, you should use the mouth-to-nose method instead.

Use Mouth-to-Mouth Method

3-15. In this best known method of rescue breathing, inflate the casualty's lungs with air from yours. You can do this by blowing air into his mouth. If the casualty is not breathing, place your hand on his forehead, and pinch his nostrils together with the thumb and index finger of the hand in use. With the same hand, exert pressure on his forehead to keep his head tilted backwards, and to maintain an open airway. With your other hand, keep your fingertips on the bony part of his lower jaw near his chin, and lift. It is best to do this under armed supervision since this is the last step before the casualty becomes Undead. (Figure 3-5).

Note: If you suspect the casualty has a neck injury and you are using the jaw-thrust technique, close his nostrils by placing your cheek tightly against them.

3-16. Take a deep breath, and seal your mouth (airtight) around the casualty's mouth (Figure 3-7). If he is small, cover both his nose and mouth with your mouth, and then seal your lips against his face.

Figure 3-7. Rescue breathing.

3-17. Blow two full breaths into the casualty's mouth (1 to 1½ seconds each), taking a fresh breath of air each time, before you blow. Watch from the corner of your eye for the casualty's chest to rise. If it does, then you are getting enough air into his lungs. If it fails to rise, then do the following:

1. Take corrective action immediately by reestablishing the airway. Ensure no air is leaking from around your mouth or from the casualty's pinched nose.
2. Try (again) to ventilate him.
3. If his chest still fails to rise, take the necessary action to open an obstructed airway.
4. If you are still unable to ventilate the casualty, reposition his head, and repeat rescue breathing. The main reason ventilation fails is improper chin and head positioning. If you cannot ventilate the casualty after you reposition his head, then move on to foreign-body airway obstruction maneuvers.
5. If, after you give two slow breaths, the casualty's chest rises, then see if you can find a pulse. A pulse is a sign of life. No pulse is a sign of undeath. Feel on the side of his neck closest to you by placing the index and middle fingers of your hand on the groove beside his Adam's apple (carotid pulse; Figure 3-8). Avoid using your thumb to take a pulse, because that could cause you to confuse your own pulse for his.
6. Maintain the airway by keeping your other hand on the casualty's forehead. Allow 5 to 10 seconds to determine if there is a pulse.
7. If you see signs of circulation and you find a pulse, and the casualty has started breathing—
   a. *Stop* and allow the casualty to breathe on his own. If possible, keep him warm and comfortable.
   b. If you find a pulse, and the casualty is unable to breathe, continue rescue breathing until told to cease by medical personnel.
   c. If you fail to find a pulse, do not take your eyes from the casualty and seek medical personnel for help as soon as possible.

Use Mouth-to-Nose Method

3-18. Use this method if you cannot perform mouth-to-mouth rescue breathing. Normally, the reason you cannot is that the casualty has a severe jaw fracture or mouth wound because his jaws are tightly closed by spasms, or in the early stages of undeath the casualty's incisors have extended and breath is foul. The mouth-to-nose method is the same as the mouth-to-mouth method, except that you blow into the *nose* while you hold the *lips* closed, keeping one hand at the chin. Then, you remove your mouth to let the casualty exhale passively. You might have to separate the casualty's liverlips to allow the air to escape during exhalation. Leave it!

Figure 3-8. Placement of fingers to detect pulse.

React to Airway Obstructions

3-19. For oxygen to flow to and from the lungs, the upper airway must be unobstructed. Upper airway obstruction can cause either partial or complete airway blockage. Upper airway obstructions often occur because—

1. The casualty's tongue falls back into his throat while he is unconscious.
2. His tongue falls back and obstructs the airway.
3. He was unable to swallow an obstruction.
4. He regurgitated the contents of his stomach, and they blocked his airway.
5. He has suffered blood clots due to head and facial injuries.

Note: *For an injured or unconscious casualty, correctly position him, and then create and maintain an open airway.*

Determine Degree of Obstruction

3-20. The airway may be partially or completely obstructed.

Partial

3-21. The person might still have an air exchange. If he has enough, then he can cough forcefully, even though he might wheeze between coughs. Instead of interfering, encourage him to cough up the object on his own. If he is not getting enough air, his coughing will be weak, and he might be making a high-pitched noise between coughs. He might also show signs of shock, which are different than signs of undeath. Help him and treat him as though he had a complete obstruction.

Complete

3-22. A complete obstruction (no air exchange) is indicated if the casualty cannot speak, breathe, or cough at all. He might clutch his neck and move erratically. In an unconscious casualty, a complete obstruction is also indicated if, after opening his airway, you cannot ventilate him.

Open Obstructed Airway, Casualty Lying Down or Unresponsive

3-23. Sometimes you must expel an airway obstruction in a casualty who is lying down, who becomes unconscious, or who is found unconscious (cause unknown; Figure 3-9):

1. If a conscious casualty, who is choking, becomes unresponsive:
    a. Call for help.
    b. Open the airway.
    c. Perform a finger sweep.
    d. Try rescue breathing. If an airway blockage prevents this,
    e. Remove the airway obstruction.
2. If a casualty is unresponsive when you find him (cause unknown):
    a. Assess or evaluate the situation.
    b. Call for help.
    c. Position the casualty on his back.
    d. Open the airway.
    e. Establish breathlessness.
    f. Try to perform rescue breathing. If still unable to ventilate the casualty,
    g. Perform six to ten manual (abdominal or chest) thrusts.

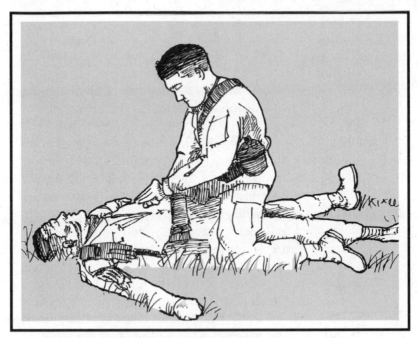

Figure 3-9. Abdominal thrust on unresponsive casualty.

3. To perform the abdominal thrusts:
   a. Kneel astride the casualty's thighs.
   b. Place the heel of one hand against the casualty's abdomen, in the midline slightly above the navel, but well below the tip of the breastbone.
   c. Place your other hand on top of the first one.
   d. Point your fingers toward the casualty's head.
   e. Use your body weight to press into the casualty's abdomen with a quick, forward and upward thrust.
   f. Deliver each thrust quickly and distinctly.
   g. Repeat the sequence of abdominal thrusts, finger sweep, and rescue breathing (try to ventilate) as long as necessary to remove the object from the obstructed airway.
   h. If the casualty's chest rises, check for a pulse.
4. To perform chest thrusts—
   a. Place the unresponsive casualty on his back, face up, and open his mouth.

b. Kneel close to his side.

c. Locate the lower edge of his ribs with your fingers.

d. Run your fingers up along the rib cage to the notch (A, Figure 3-10).

e. Place your middle finger on the notch, and your index finger next to your middle finger, on the lower edge of his breastbone.

f. Place the heel of your other hand on the lower half of his breastbone, next to your two fingers (B, Figure 3-10).

g. Remove your fingers from the notch and place that hand on top of your hand on his breastbone, extending or interlocking your fingers.

h. Straighten and lock your elbows, with your shoulders directly above your hands. Be careful to avoid bending your elbows, rocking, or letting your shoulders sag. Apply enough pressure to depress the breastbone 1½ to 2 inches, and then release the pressure completely. Repeat six to ten times. Deliver each thrust quickly and distinctly. Figure 3-11 shows another view of the breastbone being depressed.

i. Repeat the sequence of chest thrust, finger sweep, and rescue breathing as long as necessary to clear the object from the obstructed airway.

j. If the casualty's chest rises, check his pulse.

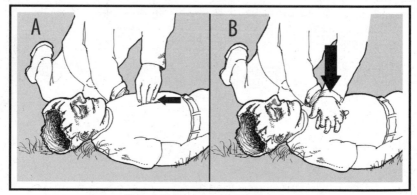

Figure 3-10. Hand placement for chest thrust.

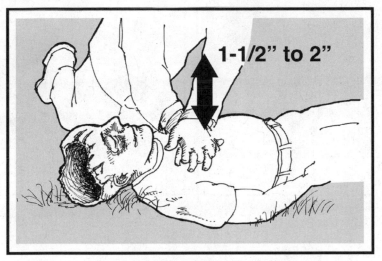

Figure 3-11. Breastbone depresses 1½ to 2 inches.

5. If you still cannot administer rescue breathing due to an airway obstruction, remove the obstruction:
   a. Place the casualty on his back, face up.
   b. Turn him all at once (avoid twisting his body).
   c. Call for help.
   d. Perform finger sweep.
   e. Keep him face up.
   f. Use the tongue-jaw lift to open his mouth.
   g. Open his mouth by grasping both his tongue and lower jaw between your thumb and fingers, and lift (tongue-jaw lift; Figure 3-12). Again, listen for groaning and watch for excessive drool and extended incisors. Abort efforts at the first signs of zombie-ism.
   h. If you cannot open his mouth, cross your fingers and thumb (crossed-finger method), and push his teeth apart. To do this, press your thumb against his upper teeth, and your finger against his lower teeth (Figure 3-13).
   i. Insert the index finger of your other hand down along the inside of his cheek to the base of his tongue. Use a hooking motion from the side of the mouth toward the center to dislodge the foreign body (Figure 3-14).

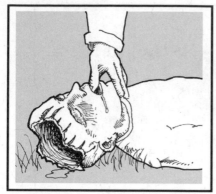

Figure 3-12. Opening of casualty's mouth, tongue-jaw lift.

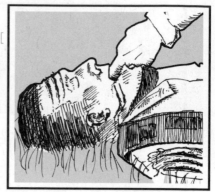

Figure 3-13. Opening of casualty's mouth, crossed-finger method.

CHECK FOR BLEEDING

Stop Bleeding and Protect Wound

3-24. The longer a Soldier bleeds from a major wound, the less likely he will survive it. (FM 4-25.11 covers first aid for open, abdominal, chest, and head wounds.) You must promptly stop the external bleeding without infecting yourself. If zombie blood (Z-positive) enters your body through a cut or cavity, you will become Undead. Use extreme caution.

Figure 3-14. Use of finger to dislodge a foreign body.

Clothing

3-25. In evaluating him for location, type, and size of wound or injury, cut or tear the casualty's clothing and carefully expose the entire area of the wound. This is necessary to properly visualize the injury and avoid further contamination. To avoid further injury, leave in place any clothing that is stuck to the wound. *Do not touch* the wound, and keep it as clean as possible.

DANGER

Take care not to force the object deeper into the airway by pushing it with your finger.

WARNING

In a toxic or chemical waste environment, leave a casualty's protective clothing in place. Apply dressings over the protective clothing.

DANGER

If a weapon lodges in the body (fails to exit), *DO NOT* try to remove it, and *DO NOT* probe the wound. Apply a dressing. If an object like a rock or splintered 2X4 is extending from (impaled in) the wound, *leave it. DO NOT* try to remove it. Instead, take the following steps to prevent further injury:

1. In order to prevent the object from embedding more deeply, or from worsening the wound, use dressings or other clean, bulky materials to build up the area around the object.
2. Apply a supporting bandage over the bulky materials to hold them in place.

Monitor the casualty continually for development of conditions that may require you to perform basic lifesaving measures, such as clearing his airway and performing mouth-to-mouth resuscitation.

Check all open (or penetrating) wounds for a point of entry and exit, with first aid measure applied accordingly.

Entrance and Exit Wounds

3-26. Before applying the dressing, carefully examine the casualty to determine if there is more than one wound. The wounds discussed here are caused by weapons. Wounds caused by bites and scratches that lead to infection will be discussed later. A stick or stake may have entered at one point and exited at another point. An exit wound is usually *larger* than its entrance wound.

Emergency Trauma Dressing

3-27. Remove the emergency bandage from the wounded Soldier's pouch (Figure 3-15). (*Do not* use the one in your pouch.)

Figure 3-15. Emergency bandage.

3-28. Place the pad on the wound, white side down, and wrap the elastic bandage around the injured limb or body part (Figure 3-16). Insert the elastic bandage into the pressure bar (Figure 3-17). Tighten the elastic bandage (Figure 3-18). Pull back, forcing the pressure bar down onto the pad (Figure 3-19). Wrap the elastic bandage tightly over the pressure bar, and wrap over all the edges of the pad (Figure 3-20). Secure the hooking ends of the closure bar into the elastic bandage. *Do not* create a tourniquet-like effect (Figure 3-21).

3-29. Remove the casualty's field dressing from the wrapper, and grasp the tails of the dressing with both hands (Figure 3-22).

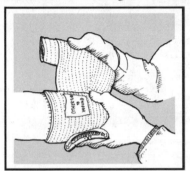
Figure 3-16. Application of pad to wound.

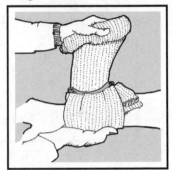
Figure 3-17. Insertion of bandage into pressure bar.

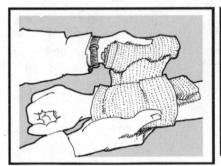
Figure 3-18. Tightening of bandage.

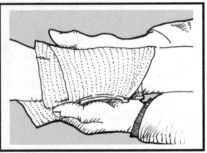
Figure 3-19. Pressure of bar into bandage.

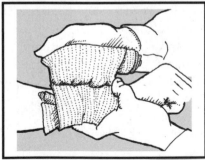
Figure 3-20. Wrapping of bandage over pressure bar.

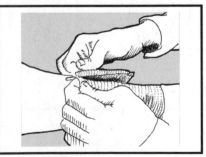
Figure 3-21. Securing of bandage.

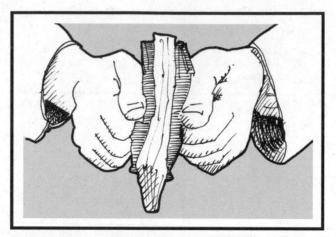

Figure 3-22. Grasping of dressing tails with both hands.

Figure 3-23.
Pulling dressing open.

3-30. Hold the dressing directly over the wound with the white side down. Open the dressing (Figure 3-23), and place it directly over the wound (Figure 3-24). Hold the dressing in place with one hand. Use the other hand to wrap one of the tails around the injured part, covering about half the dressing (Figure 3-25). Leave enough of the tail for a knot. If the casualty is able, he can help by holding the dressing in place.

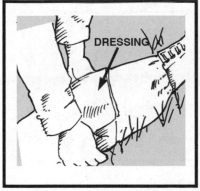

Figure 3-24. Placement of dressing directly on wound.

Figure 3-25. Wrapping of dressing tail around injured part.

3-31. Wrap the other tail in the opposite direction until the rest of the dressing is covered. The tails should seal the sides of the dressing to keep foreign material from getting under it. Tie the tails into a nonslip knot over the outer edge of the dressing (Figure 3-26). *Do not tie the knot over the wound.* In order to allow uninfected or Z-negative blood to flow to the rest of the injured limb, tie the dressing firmly enough to prevent it from slipping, but without causing a tourniquet effect. That is, the skin beyond the injury should not become cool, blue, or numb.

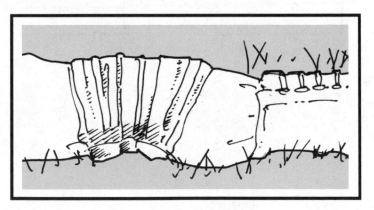

Figure 3-26. Tails tied into nonslip knot.

Manual Pressure

3-32. If bleeding continues after you apply the sterile field dressing, apply direct pressure to the dressing for five to ten minutes (Figure 3-27). If the casualty is conscious and can follow instructions, you can ask him to do this himself. Elevate an injured limb slightly above the level of the heart to reduce the bleeding (Figure 3-28).

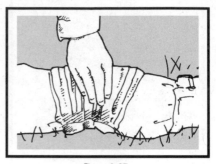

Figure 3-27.
Application of direct manual pressure.

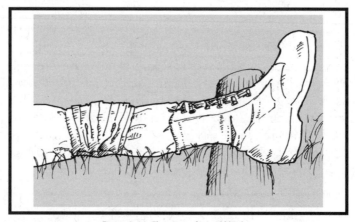

Figure 3-28. Elevation of injured limb.

WARNING

Elevate a suspected fractured limb *only after* properly splintering it.

3-33. If the bleeding stops, check for shock, and then give first aid for that as needed. If the bleeding continues, apply a pressure dressing.

Pressure Dressing

3-34. If bleeding continues after you apply a field dressing, direct pressure, and elevation, then you must apply a pressure dressing. This helps the blood clot, and it compresses the open blood vessel. Place a wad of padding on top of the field dressing directly over the wound (Figure 3-29). Keep the injured extremity elevated.

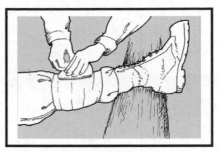

Figure 3-29.
Wad of padding on top of field dressing.

Note: Improvise bandages from strips of cloth such as tee shirts, socks, or other garments.

3-35. Place an improvised dressing (or cravat, if available) over the wad of padding (Figure 3-30). Wrap the ends tightly around the injured limb, covering the original field dressing (Figure 3-31).

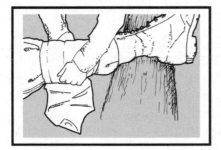

Figure 3-30.
Improvised dressing over wad of padding.

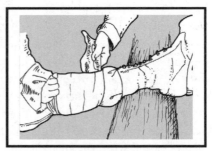

Figure 3-31.
Ends of improvised dressing wrapped tightly around limb.

3-36. Tie the ends together in a nonslip knot, directly over the wound site (Figure 3-32). *Do not* tie so tightly that it has a tourniquet-like effect. If bleeding continues and all other measures fail, or if the limb is severed, then apply a tourniquet, but do so *only as a last resort*. When the bleeding stops, check for shock, and give first aid for that, if needed.

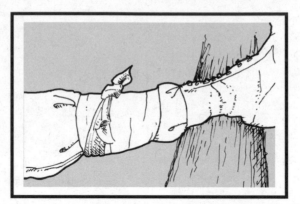
Figure 3-32. Ends of improvised dressing tied together in nonslip knot.

3-37. Check fingers and toes periodically for adequate circulation. Finger and toenails that are turning long and yellow may be an early sign of undeath. Loosen the dressing if the extremity becomes cool, blue, or numb. If bleeding continues, and all other measures fail—application of dressings, covering of wound, direct manual pressure, elevation of limb above heart level, application of pressure dressing while maintaining limb elevation—then apply digital pressure.

Digital Pressure

3-38. Use this method when you are having a hard time controlling bleeding, before you apply a pressure dressing, or where pressure dressings are unavailable. Keep the limb elevated and direct pressure on the wound. At the same time, press your fingers, thumbs, or whole hand where a main artery supplying the wounded area lies near the surface or over bone (Figure 3-33). This might help shut off, or at least slow, the flow of blood from the heart to the wound.

Tourniquet

3-39. A tourniquet is a constricting band placed around an arm or leg to control bleeding. A Soldier whose arm or leg has been completely amputated or infected might not be yellowed, bubbling, bleeding or suppurating when first discovered, but you should apply a tourniquet anyway. The body initially stops bleeding by contracting or clotting the

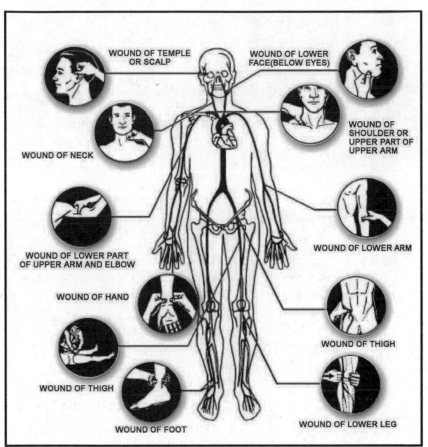

Figure 3-33. Digital pressure (fingers, thumbs, or hands).

blood vessels. However, when the vessels relax, or if a clot is knocked loose when the casualty is moved, the bleeding can restart. Bleeding from a major artery of the thigh, lower leg, or arm, and bleeding from multiple arteries, both of which occur in a traumatic amputation, might be more than you can control with manual pressure. If even under firm hand pressure the dressing gets soaked with blood, and if the wound continues to bleed, then you *must* apply a tourniquet.

3-40. Avoid using a tourniquet unless a pressure dressing fails to stop the bleeding, or unless an arm or leg has been torn off or infected. Tourniquets can injure blood vessels and nerves. Also, if left in place too long, a tourniquet can actually cause the loss of an arm or leg. However, that said, once you apply a tourniquet, you have to leave it in place and get the casualty to the nearest MTF ASAP. *Never* loosen or release a tourniquet yourself after you have applied one, because that could cause severe bleeding and lead to shock.

Zombie Application Tourniquet

1. The ZAT is packaged for one-handed use. Slide the wounded extremity through the loop of the ZAT tape (1, Figure 3-34).
2. Position the ZAT 2 inches above a bleeding, yellowing, suppurating site that is above the knee or elbow. Pull the free

running end of the tape tight, and fasten it securely back on itself (2, Figure 3-34).

3. Do not affix the band past the windlass clip (3, Figure 3-34).
4. Twist the windlass rod until the bleeding or oozing stops (4, Figure 3-34).
5. Lock the rod in place with the windlass clip (5, Figure 3-34).
6. For small extremities, continue to wind the tape around the extremity and over the windlass rod (6, Figure 3-34).
7. Grasp the windlass strap, pull it tight, and adhere it to the hook-pile tape on the windlass clip (7, Figure 3-34). The ZAT is now ready for transport.

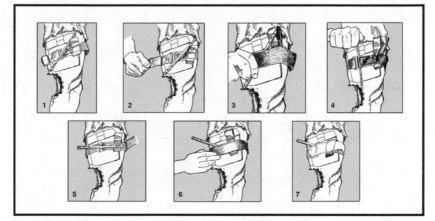

Figure 3-34. Zombie application tourniquet.

WARNING

The one-handed method for upper extremities may not be completely effective on lower extremities. Ensure everyone receives familiarization and training on both methods of application.

3-41. The zombie first-aid kit (ZFAK) allows self-aid and buddy aid (SABA) interventions for extremity hemorrhages and airway compromises suffered in combat with the Undead (Figure 3-35). The pouch and insert are both Class II items. Expendables are Class VIII. While similar to the improved first-aid kit (IFAK), the ZFAK also contains the Zombie Application Tourniquet (ZAT), Anti-Zombie Virus Gloves, Zombix, and special Zombie Dressing.

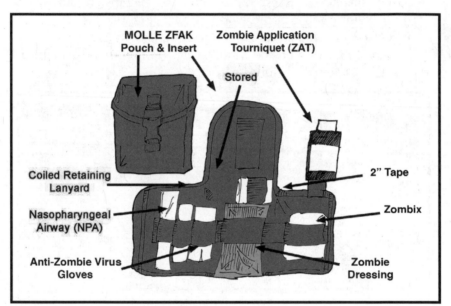

Figure 3-35. Improved zombie first aid kit.

Improvised Tourniquet

3-42. In the absence of a specially designed tourniquet, you can make one from any strong, pliable material such as gauze or muslin bandages, clothing, or cravats. Use your improvised tourniquet with a rigid, stick-like object. To minimize skin damage, the improvised tourniquet must be at least 2-inches wide.

Placement

3-43. To position the makeshift tourniquet, place it around the limb, between the wound and the body trunk, or between the wound and the heart. *Never* place it directly over a wound, a fracture, or joint. For maximum effectiveness, place it on the upper arm or above the knee on the thigh (Figure 3-36).

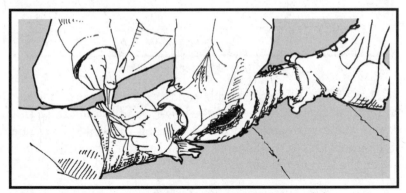

Figure 3-36. Tourniquet above knee.

3-44. Pad the tourniquet well. If possible, place it over a smoothed sleeve or trouser leg to keep the skin from being pinched or twisted. If the tourniquet is long enough, wrap it around the limb several times, keeping the material as flat as possible. Damaging the skin may deprive the surgeon of skin required to cover an amputation. Protecting the skin also reduces the casualty's pain.

Application

3-45. To apply the tourniquet, tie a half knot, which is the same as the first part of tying a shoe lace. Place a stick, or other rigid object, on top of the half knot (Figure 3-37).

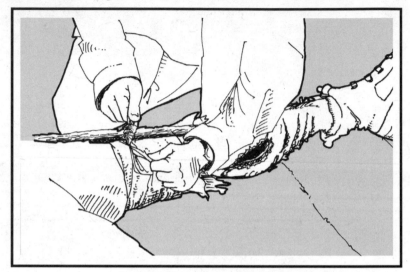

Figure 3-37. Rigid object on top of half knot.

3-46. Tie a full-knot over the stick, and twist the stick until the tourniquet tightens around the limb or the bright red bleeding stops (Figure 3-38). In the case of amputation, dark oozing blood may continue for a short time. This is the infected z-positive blood trapped in the area between the wound and tourniquet.

3-47. To fasten the tourniquet to the limb, loop the free ends of the tourniquet over the ends of the stick. Bring the ends around the limb to keep the stick from loosening. Tie the ends together on the side of the limb (Figure 3-39).

3-48. You can use other means to secure the stick. Just make sure the material remains wound around the stick and that no further injury is possible. If possible, save and transport any severed (amputated) limbs or body parts with (but out of sight of) the casualty. Never cover the tourniquet. Leave it in full view. If the limb is missing (has been completely

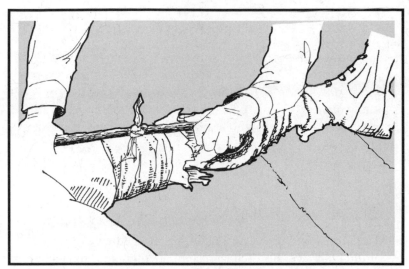

Figure 3-38. Tourniquet knotted over rigid object and twisted.

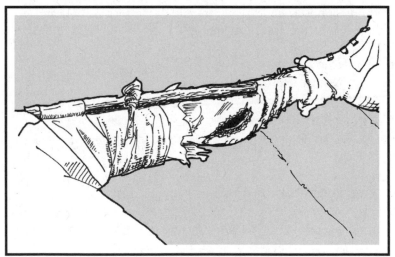

Figure 3-39. Free ends tied on side of limb.

torn or gnawed off), apply a dressing to the stump. All wounds should have a dressing to protect the wound from contamination. Mark the casualty's forehead with a "T" and the time to show that he has a tourniquet. If necessary, use the casualty's blood to make this mark. Check and treat for shock, and then seek medical aid.

CAUTION

Do not remove a tourniquet yourself. Only trained medical personnel may adjust or otherwise remove or release the tourniquet, and then only in the appropriate setting. Removing a tourniquet suddenly can result in an explosion of infected blood squirting in every direction, contaminating the environment and putting others at risk.

SHOCK

3-49. The term *shock* means various things. In medicine, it means a collapse of the body's cardiovascular system, including an inadequate supply of blood to the body's tissues. Shock stuns and weakens the Living body. Shock is the first phase of undeath. When the normal blood flow in the body is upset, undeath can result. Early recognition and proper first aid may save the casualty's life.

Causes and Effects of Shock

3-50. The three basic effects of shock are:
- Heart is damaged and fails to pump.
- Blood loss (heavy bleeding) depletes fluids in vascular system.
- Blood vessels dilate (open wider), dropping blood pressure to dangerous level.

3-51. Shock might be caused by:
- Dehydration.
- Allergic reaction to foods, drugs, insect stings, and snakebites.
- Significant loss of blood.
- Reaction to sight of a flesh wound, blood, pus, or other traumatic scene.
- Traumatic injuries.
- Burns.
- Bites, torn-off or gnawed-off limbs.
- Crush injuries.

- Blows to the body, which can break bones or damage internal organs.
- Head injuries.
- Penetrating wounds such as from teeth, stick, nailed-through 2x4.

Signs and Symptoms of Shock and Early Undeath

3-52. Examine the casualty to see if he has any of the following signs and symptoms:

- Sweaty but cool (clammy) skin.
- Weak and rapid pulse.
- (Too) rapid breathing or droning.
- Pale, gray, chalky skin tone.
- Cyanosis (blue) blotchy, peeling, or bubbling skin, especially around the mouth and lips.
- Restlessness or nervousness.
- Thirst.
- Significant loss of blood.
- Confusion or disorientation. Moving with hands extended, limping.
- Nausea, vomiting, or both.
- Bad breath.

First-Aid Measures for Shock

3-53. First-aid procedures for shock in the field are the same ones performed to prevent it. When treating a casualty, always assume the casualty is in shock, or will be shortly. Waiting until the signs of shock are visible could jeopardize the casualty's life.

Casualty Position

3-54. *Never* move the casualty, or his limbs, if you suspect he has fractures, and they have not yet been splinted. If you have cover and the situation permits, move the casualty to cover. Lay him on his back. A casualty in shock from a flesh wound, or who is having trouble breathing, might breathe easier sitting up. If so, let him sit up, but monitor him carefully, in case his condition worsens. Elevate his feet higher than the level of his heart. Support his feet with a stable object, such as a field pack or rolled up clothing, to keep them from slipping off.

3-55. Loosen clothing at the neck, waist, or wherever it might be binding.

3-56. Prevent the casualty from chilling or overheating. The key is to maintain normal body temperature. In cold weather, place a blanket or like item over and under him to keep him warm and prevent chilling. However, if a tourniquet has been applied, leave it exposed (if possible). In hot weather, place the casualty in the shade and protect him from becoming chilled; however, avoid the excessive use of blankets or other coverings. Calm the casualty. Throughout the entire procedure of providing first aid for a casualty, you should reassure the casualty and keep him calm. This can be done by being authoritative (taking charge) and by showing self-confidence. Assure the casualty that you are there to help him. Seek medical aid.

Food and Drink

3-57. When providing first aid for shock, *never* give the casualty food or drink. If you must leave the casualty, or if he is unconscious, turn his head to the side to prevent him from choking if he vomits.

3-58. Continue to evaluate the casualty until medical personnel arrives or the casualty is transported to an MTF.

CASUALTY EVACUATION

3-59. Medical evacuation of the sick and wounded (with en route medical care) is the responsibility of medical personnel who have been provided special training and equipment. Therefore, wait for some means of medical evacuation to be provided unless a good reason for you to transport a casualty arises. When the situation is urgent and you are unable to obtain medical assistance or know that no medical evacuation assets are available, you will have to transport the casualty. For this reason, you must know how to transport him without increasing the seriousness of his condition.

3-60. Transport by litter is safer and more comfortable for a casualty than manual carries. It is also easier for you as the bearer(s). However, manual transportation might be the only feasible method, due to the terrain or combat situation. You might have to do it to save a life. As soon as you can, transfer the casualty to a litter as soon as you find or can improvise one.

MANUAL CARRIES

3-61. When you carry a casualty manually, you must handle him carefully and correctly to prevent more serious or possibly fatal injuries. Situation permitting, organize the transport of the casualty, and avoid rushing. Perform each movement as deliberately *and gently* as possible. Avoid moving a casualty until the type and extent of his injuries are evaluated, and the required first aid administered. Sometimes, you will have to move the casualty immediately, for example, when he is trapped in a burning vehicle. Manual carries are tiring and can increase the severity of the casualty's injury, but might be required to save his life. Two-man carries are preferred, because they provide more comfort to the casualty, are less likely to aggravate his injuries, and are less tiring for the bearers. How far you can carry a casualty depends on many factors, such as:

- Nature of the casualty's injuries.
- Your (the bearer's or bearers') strength and endurance.
- Weight of the casualty.
- Obstacles encountered during transport (natural or manmade).
- Type of terrain.
- Pursuit by the Undead.

ONE-MAN CARRIES

3-62. Use these carries when only one bearer is available to transport the casualty:

Fireman's Carry

3-63. This is one of the easiest ways for one person to carry another. After an unconscious or disabled casualty has been properly positioned (rolled onto his abdomen), raise him from the ground, and then support him and place him in the carrying position (Figure 3-40). Here's what you do:

A. Position the casualty by rolling him onto his abdomen and straddle him. Extend your hands under his chest and lock them together (A, Figure 3-40).

B. Lift him to his knees as you move backward (B, Figure 3-40).

C. Continue to move backward, straightening his legs and locking his knees (C, Figure 3-40).

D. Walk forward, bringing him to a standing position. Tilt him slightly backward to keep his knees from buckling (D, Figure 3-40).

E. Keep supporting him with one arm, and then free your other arm, quickly grasp his wrist, and raise his arm high. Immediately pass your head under his raised arm, releasing the arm as you pass under it (E, Figure 3-40).

F. Move swiftly to face the casualty and secure your arms around his waist. Immediately place your foot between his feet, and spread them apart about 6 to 8 inches (F, Figure 3-40).

G. Grasp the casualty's wrist, and raise his arm high over your head (G, Figure 3-40).

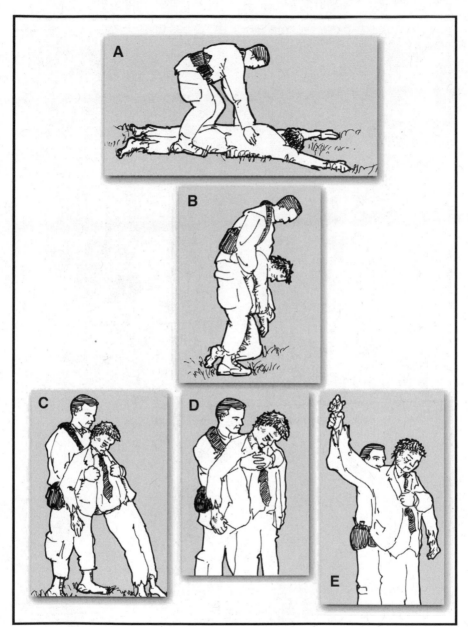

Figure 3-40. Fireman's carry.

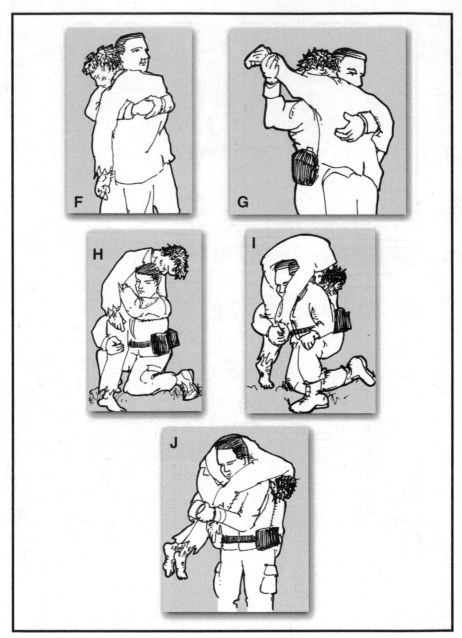

Figure 3-40. Fireman's carry (continued).

H. Bend down and pull the casualty's arm over and down on your shoulder, bringing his body across your shoulders. At the same time, pass your arm between his legs (H, Figure 3-40).

I. Grasp the casualty's wrist with one hand, and place your other hand on your knee for support (I, Figure 3-40).

J. Rise with the casualty positioned correctly. Your other hand should be free (J, Figure 3-40).

Alternate Fireman's Carry

3-64. Use this carry only when you think it is safer due to the location of the casualty's wounds. When you use the alternate carry, take care to keep the casualty's head from snapping back and injuring his neck. You can also use this method to raise a casualty from the ground for other one-man carries. First, kneel on both knees at the casualty's head and face his feet. Extend your hands under his armpits, down his sides, and across his back (A, Figure 3-41). Second, as you rise, lift the casualty to his knees. Then secure a lower hold and raise him to a standing position with his knees locked (B, Figure 3-41).

Figure 3-41. Alternate fireman's carry.

Supporting Carry

3-65. With this method (Figure 3-42), the casualty must be able to walk or at least hop on one leg, with you as a crutch. You can use this carry to help him go as far as he can walk or hop. Raise him from the ground to a standing position using the fireman's carry. Grasp his wrist, and draw his arm around your neck. Place your arm around his waist. This should enable the casualty to walk or hop, with you as a support.

Neck Drag

3-66. This method (Figure 3-43) is useful in battle, because you can carry the casualty behind a low wall or shrubbery, under a vehicle, or through a culvert. If the casualty is conscious, let him clasp his hands together around your neck. To do this, first tie his hands together

Figure 3-42. Supporting carry.

at the wrists, and then straddle him. You should be kneeling, facing the casualty. Second, loop his tied hands over and around your neck. Third, crawl forward and drag the casualty with you. If he is unconscious, protect his head from the ground.

WARNING

Avoid using this carry if the casualty has a devoured arm.

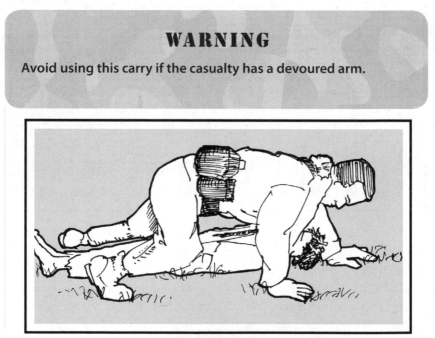

Figure 3-43. Neck drag.

Cradle-Drop Drag

3-67. Use this method to move a casualty up or down steps. Kneel at the casualty's head (with him on his back). Slide your hands, with palms up, under the casualty's shoulders. Get a firm hold under his armpits (A, Figure 3-44). Rise partially while supporting the casualty's head on one of your forearms (B, Figure 3-44). You may bring your elbows together and let the casualty's head rest on both of your forearms. Rise and drag the casualty backward so he is in a semi-seated position (C, Figure 3-44).

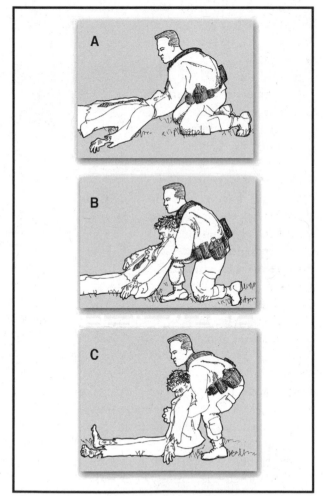

Figure 3-44. Cradle-drop drag.

TWO-MAN CARRIES

3-68. Use these when you can. They are more comfortable to the casualty, less likely to aggravate his injuries, and less tiring for you.

Two-Man Support Carry

3-69. Use this method to transport either conscious or unconscious casualties. If the casualty is taller than you (the bearers), you might have to lift his legs and let them rest on your forearms. Help him to his feet, and then support him with your arms around his waist. Then, grasp the casualty's wrists and draw his arms around your necks (Figure 3-45).

Two-Man Fore-and-Aft Carry

3-70. You can use this to transport a casualty for a long distance, say, over 300 meters. The taller of you (the two bearers) should be positioned at the casualty's head.

3-71. The shorter of you spreads the casualty's legs and kneels between them, with your back to the casualty. Position your hands behind the casualty's knees. The taller of you kneels at the casualty's head, slides your hands

Figure 3-45. Two-man support carry.

under his arms and across his chest, and locks your hands together (A, Figure 3-46). Both of you should rise together, lifting the casualty (B, Figure 3-46). If you alter this carry so that both of you are facing the casualty, you can use it to place him on a litter.

Two-Hand Seat Carry

3-72. You can use this method to carry a casualty for a short distance or to place him on a litter. With the casualty lying on his back, one of you should kneel on one side of the casualty at his hips, and the other should kneel on the other side (A, Figure 3-47). Each of you should pass your arms under the casualty's thighs and back, and grasp the other bearer's wrists. Both of you then rise, lifting the casualty (B, Figure 3-47).

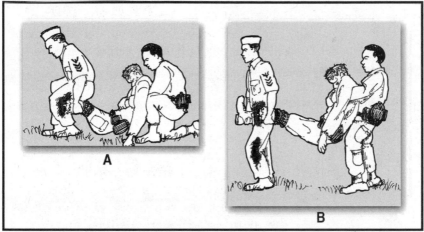

Figure 3-46. Two-man fore-and-aft carry.

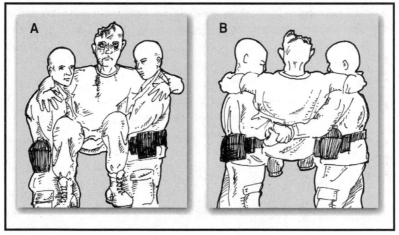

Figure 3-47. Two-hand seat carry.

IMPROVISED LITTERS

3-73. Two men can support or carry a casualty without equipment for only short distances. By using available materials to improvise equipment, two or more rescuers can transport the casualty over greater distances.

1. Sometimes, a casualty must be moved without a standard litter. The distance might be too great for a manual carry, or the casualty might have an injury, such as a bitten neck, torn back, smashed hip, or thigh, that manual transportation would aggravate. If this happens, improvise a litter from materials at hand. Construct it well to avoid dropping or further injuring the casualty. An improvised litter is an emergency measure only. Replace it with a standard litter as soon as you can.

2. You can improvise many types of litters, depending on the materials available. You can make a satisfactory litter by securing poles inside such items as ponchos, tarps, jackets, or shirts. You can improvise poles from strong branches, tent supports, skis, lengths of pipe, or other objects. If nothing is available to use as a pole, then roll a poncho or similar item from both sides toward the center, so you can grip the roll(s) and carry the casualty. You can use most any flat-surfaced object as long as it is the right size, for example, doors, boards, window shutters, benches, ladders, cots, or chairs. Try to find something to pad the litter for the casualty's comfort. You can use either the two-man fore-and-aft carry (Figure 3-46) or the two-hand seat carry (Figure 3-47) to place the casualty on a litter.

3. Use either two or four service members (head/foot) to lift a litter. Everybody should raise the litter at the same time to keep the casualty as level as possible.

DANGER

Unless there is an immediate life-threatening situation (such as a burning meteorite or nuclear power explosion), NEVER move a casualty who has a suspected back or neck injury. Instead, seek medical personnel for guidance on how to transport him.

WARNING

Use caution when transporting on a sloping incline/hill.

SECTION II. PREVENTATIVE MEDICINE

Personal hygiene and cleanliness practices (Figure 3-48) safeguard your health and that of others. Specifically, they:

- Protect against disease-causing germs that are present in all environments.
- Keep disease-causing germs from spreading.

- Never consume foods and beverages from unauthorized sources.
- Never soil the ground with urine or feces. Use a latrine or "cat hole."
- Keep your fingers and contaminated objects out of your mouth.
- Wash your hands—
  - — After any contamination.
  - — Before eating or preparing food.
  - — Before cleaning your mouth and teeth.
- Wash all mess gear after each meal or use disposable plasticware once.
- Clean your mouth and teeth at least once each day.
- Avoid insect bites by wearing proper clothing and using insect repellents.
- Avoid getting wet or chilled unnecessarily.
- Avoid sharing personal items with other Soldiers, for example—
  - — Canteens.
  - — Pipes.
  - — Toothbrushes.
  - — Washcloths.
  - — Towels.
  - — Shaving gear.
- Avoid leaving food scraps lying around.
- Sleep when possible.
- Exercise regularly.

Figure 3-48. Rules for avoiding illness in the field.

- Promote health among Soldiers.
- Improve morale.
- Repel the Undead.

CLOTHING AND SLEEPING GEAR

3-74. Situation permitting, wash or exchange your clothing when it gets dirty. Do the same with your sleeping gear. When you cannot do this, at least shake everything out and air it regularly in the sun. This will reduce the number of germs on them.

CARE OF THE FEET

3-75. Wash and dry your feet at least daily. Use foot powder on your feet to help kill germs, reduce friction on the skin, and absorb perspiration. Change your socks daily. As soon as you can after you cross a wet area, dry your feet, put on foot powder, and change socks (Figure 3-49). Also note that the Undead take no such preventative measures and thus are often filthy, germ-ridden, barefoot, and lack morale.

Figure 3-49. Care of the feet.

FOOD AND DRINK

3-76. For proper development, strength, and survival, your body requires proteins, fats, and carbo-hydrates. While the Undead subsist on a diet of mostly human flesh, brains, and the occasional barn cat or mouse, a Soldier must maintain a well-balanced, healthy diet. Your diet requires minerals, vitamins, and water. Issued rations have those essential food substances in the right amounts and proper balance. So, primarily eat those rations. When feasible, heat your meals. This will make them taste better and will reduce the energy required to digest them. Avoid overindulging in sweets, soft drinks, alcoholic beverages, and other non-issued rations. They have little nutritional value, and are often harmful. Eat food only from approved sources. Drink water only from approved sources, or treat it with water purification tablets.

MENTAL HEALTH AND MORALE

3-77. To maintain mental health and self-confidence:

MENTAL HYGIENE
3-78. The way you think affects the way you act. If you know your job, you will probably act quickly and effectively. If you are uncertain or doubtful of your ability to do your job, you may hesitate and make wrong decisions. Positive thinking is a necessity. You must enter combat with absolute confidence in your ability to do your job. Keep in mind that:

- Fear is a basic human emotion. It is mental and physical. In itself, fear is not shameful, if controlled. It can even help you, by making you more alert and more able to do your job. For example, a fear-induced adrenaline rush might help you respond and defend yourself or your comrades quickly during an unpredicted event or combat situation. Therefore, fear can help you—use it to your advantage.
- Avoid letting your imagination and fear run wild. Dismiss urban legends and most horror movies. They are not real. Combat however, is real. Also remember, you are not alone. You are part of a team. Other Soldiers are nearby, even though you cannot always see them. Everyone must help each other and depend on each other.
- Worry undermines the body, dulls the mind, and slows thinking and learning. It adds to confusion, magnifies troubles, and causes you to imagine things that really do not exist. If you are worried about something, talk to your leader about it. He might be able to help solve the problem.
- You might have to fight in any part of the world and in all types of terrain. Therefore, adjust your mind to accept conditions as they are. If mentally prepared for it, you should be able to fight under almost any conditions.

EXERCISE

3-79. Exercise your muscles and joints to maintain your physical fitness and good health. Strength is a powerful weapon against the Undead, which are persistent but physically weak. Without exercise, you might lack the physical stamina and ability to fight. Physical fitness includes a healthy body, the capacity for skillful and sustained performance, the ability to recover from exertion rapidly, the desire to complete a designated task, and the confidence to face any possible event. Your own safety, health, and life may depend on your physical fitness. During lulls in combat, counteract inactivity by exercising. This helps keep your muscles and body functions ready for the next period of combat. It also helps pass the time.

REST

3-80. Just as your Undead enemy returns each morning to their graves to recharge, you too must rest. Your body needs regular periods of rest to restore physical and mental vigor. When you are tired, your body functions are like those of the Undead: sluggish, and your ability to react is slower than normal, which makes you more susceptible to sickness, and to making errors that could endanger you or others. For the best health, you should get 6 to 8 hours of uninterrupted sleep each day. As that is seldom possible in combat, use rest periods and off-duty time to rest or sleep. Never be ashamed to say that you are tired or sleepy. However, *never* sleep on duty.

CHAPTER 4

ENVIRONMENTAL CONDITIONS

The infiltration of the Undead into all cultures means that today's Soldier must be ready to deploy and fight anywhere in the world. Corpses rise from the dead in every environment, and so Soldiers for the Living may go into the tropical heat of Central America, the deserts of the Middle East, and the frozen tundra of Alaska. Each environment presents unique situations concerning a Soldier's performance. Furthermore, physical exertion in extreme environments can be life threatening. While recognizing such problems are important, preventing them is even more important; and furthermore, requires an understanding of the environmental factors that affect the performance of the Living Soldier and the Undead enemy and how the body responds to those factors.

SECTION I. DESERT

Desert terrain, demanding and difficult to traverse, often provides very few landmarks. Furthermore, with cover and concealment highly limited, the threat of exposure to the Undead is constant. Most arid areas have several types of terrain and like the wildlife native to these areas, each environment hosts zombies particularly well adapted to their specific region. While deserts are sometimes seen as devoid of undeath, the opposite is true. The desert has long attracted meteorites, UFOs, nuclear facilities and testing sites, nomadic religious sects and cults, unmarked roadside graves, and secret government organizations. History tells us that wherever such things are found, the Undead are never far away.

TYPES

4-1. The five basic desert types are:

- Mountainous (high altitude).
- Rocky plateaus.
- Sand dunes.
- Salt marshes.
- Broken, dissected terrain (*gebels* or *wadis*).

MOUNTAINOUS DESERTS

4-2. Scattered ranges or areas of barren hills or mountains separated by dry, flat basins characterize mountainous deserts. High ground may rise gradually or abruptly from flat areas to several thousand meters above sea level. Most of the infrequent rainfall occurs on high ground and runs off rapidly in the form of flash floods. These floodwaters erode deep gullies and ravines, and deposit sand and gravel around the edges of the basins. Water rapidly evaporates, leaving the land as barren as before, although there may be short-lived vegetation. The Undead in mountainous deserts have developed tough feet, strong legs, thicker skin, the occasional beard, and a forward slouch that is even more pronounced than usual. They have also developed stamina and are harder targets than you will find in the lowlands.

ROCKY PLATEAU DESERTS

4-3. Rocky plateau deserts have relatively slight relief interspersed with extensive flat areas with quantities of solid or broken rock at or near the surface. There may be steep-walled, eroded valleys, known as *wadis* in the Middle East and *arroyos* or canyons in the US and Mexico. Although their flat bottoms may be superficially attractive as assembly areas, the narrower valleys can be extremely dangerous to men and material due to flash flooding after rains. The Undead here resemble those described in section 4-2. They are strong and hearty, though zombies found in plateau deserts often stand more upright and thus can move faster across the plain. Should they attack, you will have less reaction time than with the Undead described in 4-2.

SAND DUNES

4-4. Sand dune deserts are extensive flat areas covered with sand or gravel. "Flat" is a relative term, as some areas may contain sand dunes that are over 1,000 feet (300 meters) high and 10 to 15 miles (16 to 24 kilometers) long. Traffic ability in such terrain will depend on the windward or leeward slope of the dunes and the texture of the sand. However, other areas may be flat for 10,000 feet (3,000 meters) and more. Zombies here—often referred to by Special Forces veterans as "Retirement Communities"–exist in small groups where hot, dry weather keep the Undead looking the opposite of those found in the mountains or swamps. They tend not to have the moisture issues (drool, phlegm, stink) of their cousins. Some still have hair. Their dead skin, rather than being white or gray, reaches a pasty golden brown.

SALT MARSHES

4-5. Salt marshes are flat, desolate areas sometimes studded with clumps of grass, but devoid of other vegetation. They occur in arid areas where rainwater .has collected, evaporated, and left large deposits of alkali salts and water with a high salt concentration. The water is so salty it is undrinkable. A crust that may be 1- to 12-inches (2.5- to 30-centimeters) thick forms over the saltwater. Arid areas may contain salt marshes as many as hundreds of kilometers square. These areas usually support many insects, most of which bite. The corrosive atmosphere of salt marshes gives the zombies here the worst complexions of any you will find. The Undead here often wander naked and shoeless, with large patches of skin altogether missing. One Special Forces veteran with experience in Salt Marsh battle said the faces of the Undead resemble "cheese pizza with the cheese pulled off."

BROKEN AND DISSECTED TERRAIN

4-6. All arid areas contain broken or highly dissected terrain. Rainstorms that erode soft sand and carve out canyons form this terrain. A wade may range from 10 feet (3 meters) wide and 7 feet (2 meters) deep to several hundred meters wide and deep. The direction a wade takes varies as much as its width and depth. It twists and turns in a maze-like pattern. A wade will give you good cover and concealment, but be cautious when deciding to try to move through it, because it is very difficult terrain to negotiate. Zombies found here have the combined traits of the other desert zombies, and are thus hearty and tough. Be careful.

PREPARATION

4-7. Surviving in an arid area depends on what you know and how prepared you are for the environmental conditions.

FACTORS
4-8. In a desert area, you must consider:

- Low rainfall.
- Intense sunlight and heat.
- Wide temperature range.
- Sparse vegetation.
- High mineral content near ground surface.
- Sandstorms.
- Mirages, including mirages of the Undead that can be hard to distinguish from the real thing.

Low Rainfall
4-9. Low rainfall is the most obvious environmental factor in an arid area. Some desert areas receive less than 4 inches (10 centimeters) of rain annually. When they do, it comes as brief torrents that quickly run off the ground surface.

Intense Sunlight And Heat
4-10. Intense sunlight and heat are present in all arid areas. Air temperature can rise as high as 140° F (60° C) during the day. Heat gain results from direct sunlight, hot blowing sand-laden winds, reflective heat (the

sun's rays bouncing off the sand), and conductive heat from direct contact with the desert sand and rock. Intense sunlight and heat increase the body's need for water. Radios and sensitive equipment items exposed to direct intense sunlight could malfunction.

Wide Temperature Range

4-11. Temperatures in arid areas may get as high as 130° F (55° C) during the day, and as low as 50° F (10° C) at night. The drop in temperature at night occurs rapidly and will chill a person who lacks warm clothing and is unable to move about. The cool evenings and nights are the best times to work or travel, though the Undead favor this time of day for the same reasons. Thus, desert encounters and battle often take place at night.

Sparse Vegetation

4-12. Vegetation is sparse in arid areas; therefore, you will have trouble finding shelter and camouflaging your movements. During daylight hours, large areas of terrain are easily visible. If traveling in hostile territory, follow the principles of desert camouflage:

- Hide or seek shelter in dry washes (*wades*) with thick vegetation and cover from oblique observation.
- Use the shadows cast from brush, rocks, or outcroppings. The temperature in shaded areas will be 52 to 63º F (11 to 17º C) cooler than the air temperature.
- Cover objects that will reflect the light from the sun.

4-13. Before moving, survey the area for sites that provide cover and concealment. Keep in mind that it will be difficult to estimate distance. The emptiness of desert terrain causes most people to underestimate distance by a *factor of three*: a zombie appearing to be ½ mile (1 kilometer) away is really 1.75 miles (3 kilometers) away.

Sandstorms

4-14. Sandstorms (sand-laden winds) occur frequently in most deserts. The greatest danger is getting lost in a swirling wall of sand and encountering your Undead enemy at close range. Because sand retards sight, sound, and smell, you can literally run into a zombie during a storm. Wear goggles and cover your mouth and nose with cloth. If natural shelter is unavailable, mark your direction of travel, lie down, and wait out the storm. Dust and wind-blown sand interfere with radio transmissions. Therefore, plan to use other means of signaling such as pyrotechnics, signal mirrors, or marker panels, whichever you have.

Mirages

4-15. Mirages are optical phenomena caused by the refraction of light through heated air rising from a sandy or stony surface. Mirages occur in the desert's interior about 6 miles (10 kilometers) from the coast. They make objects that are 1 mile (1.5 kilometers) or more away appear to move. This mirage effect makes it difficult for you to identify an object from a distance. It also blurs distant range contours so much that you feel surrounded by a sheet of water from which elevations stand out as "islands." The mirage effect makes it hard for a person to identify targets, estimate range, and see objects clearly. However, if you can get to high ground (10 feet [3 meters] or more above the desert floor), you can get above the superheated air close to the ground and overcome the mirage effect. Mirages make land navigation difficult, because they obscure natural features. Do not survey the area from dusk till dawn. Survey at dawn, dusk, or by moonlight when there is little likelihood of mirage. Light levels in desert areas are more intense than in other geographic areas. Moonlit nights are usually clear, with excellent visibility, because daytime winds die down and haze and glare disappear. You can see torches, lights, red flashlights, and blackout lights at great distances. Sound carries very far as well. Conversely, during nights with little moonlight, visibility is extremely poor. Traveling is extremely hazardous. You must avoid getting lost, falling into ravines, or stumbling into Undead positions. Movement during such a night is practical only if you have a means to determine direction and have spent the day resting; observing and memorizing the terrain; and selecting your route.

NEED FOR WATER

4-16. Since the early days of World War II, when the Special Forces were preparing to fight the Undead near the uranium mines of North

Africa, the subject of Soldier and water in the desert has generated considerable interest and confusion. At one time, the US Army thought it could condition men to do with less water by progressively reducing their water supplies during training. This practice of water discipline resulted in slow, sluggish behavior of overheated troops and numerous victories for the Undead. A key factor in desert survival is understanding the relationship between physical activity, air temperature, and water consumption. The body requires a certain amount of water for a certain level of activity at a certain temperature. For example, a person performing hard work in the sun at 109° F (43° C) requires 19 liters (5 gallons) of water daily. Lack of the required amount of water causes a rapid decline in an individual's ability to make decisions and to perform tasks efficiently. Understanding how the air temperature and your physical activity affect your water requirements allows you to take measures to get the most from your water supply. These measures are:

- Find shade and get out of the sun!
- Place something between you and the hot ground.
- Limit your movements!
- Conserve your sweat. Wear your complete uniform to include T-shirt. Roll the sleeves down, cover your head, and protect your neck with a scarf or similar item. Your clothing will absorb your sweat, keeping it against your skin so that you gain its full cooling effect.

4-17. Thirst is not a reliable guide for your need for water. A person who uses thirst as a guide will drink only two thirds of his daily water requirement. Drinking water at regular intervals helps your body remain cool and decreases sweating:

- Below 100° F (38° C), drink 0.5 liter (2 cups) of water every hour.
- Above 100° F (38° C), drink 1 liter (4 cups) of water every hour.

HAZARDS
4-18. Several hazards are unique to the desert environment. These include insects, snakes, thorny plants and cacti, contaminated water, sunburn, eye irritation, and climatic stress. Man, as a source of water and food,

attracts lice, mites, wasps, and flies. Insects are extremely unpleasant and may carry diseases. Old buildings, ruins, and caves are favorite habitats of spiders, scorpions, centipedes, lice, and mites, all of which also make their home on the Undead, which make easy hosts due to their poor immune systems and nonaggressive nature toward nonhumans. These areas provide protection from the elements and attract other wildlife. Therefore, take extra care when staying in these areas. Wear gloves at all times in the desert. Do not place your hands anywhere without first looking to see what is there. Visually inspect an area before sitting or lying down. When you get up, shake out and inspect your boots and clothing. All desert areas have snakes. They inhabit ruins, native villages, garbage dumps, caves, and natural rock outcroppings that offer shade, and yes, the Undead. Thus, never step barefoot or walk near the Undead without carefully inspecting them for snakes. Pay attention to where you place your feet and hands. Most snakebites result from stepping on or handling snakes. Once you see a snake emerge from a zombie (often from an eye socket), for example, give it a wide berth.

SECTION II. JUNGLE

The jungle comprises a substantial portion of the earth's land mass and hosts a surprising number of the Undead. Jungle environments consist of tall grasslands; mountains; swamps; blue and brown water; and single/double-canopy vegetation. Jungle environments are prominent in South America, Asia, and Africa. High temperatures, heavy rainfall, and oppressive humidity characterize equatorial and subtropical regions, except at high altitudes. At low altitudes, temperature variation is seldom less than 50° F (10° C) and is often more than 95° F (35° C). At high altitudes, ice often forms at night. Violent storms occur, usually toward the end of summer. The dry season has rain once a day and the monsoon has continuous rain. Day and night are of equal length. Darkness falls quickly and daybreak is just as sudden. In tropical forest areas, reports suggest that zombies are produced by shamans of native religions. A less likely cause of corpse reanimation is seepage of rainwater into the soil of burial grounds. This rainwater absorbs the powerful medicinal chemicals from native plant life as it falls to the ground, and is allegedly capable of raising the dead. If not the cause of reanimation, chemically loaded rainwater ensures healthy, powerful zombies. Leaders must consider several jungle subtypes and other factors when performing duty and surviving in the jungle.

TYPES

4-19. There is no standard type of jungle. Jungle can consist of any combination of the following terrain subtypes, all of which contain zombies unique to the terrain:

- Rain forests.
- Secondary jungles.
- Semi-evergreen seasonal and monsoon forests.
- Scrub and thorn forests.
- Savannas.
- Saltwater swamps.
- Freshwater swamps.

TROPICAL RAIN FORESTS

4-20. The climate varies little in rain forests. You find these forests across the equator in the Amazon and Congo basins, parts of Indonesia, and several Pacific islands. Up to 144 inches (365.8 centimeters) of rain falls throughout the year. Temperatures range from about 90° F (32° C) in the day to 70° F (21° C) at night. There are five layers of vegetation in this jungle. Sometimes still untouched by Living humans, jungle trees rise from buttress roots to heights of 198 feet (60 meters). Below them, smaller trees produce a canopy so thick that little light reaches the jungle floor. Ferns, mosses, and herbaceous plants push through a thick carpet of leaves, and fungi adorn leaves and fallen trees. The darkness of the jungle floor limits growth, which aids in movement, but dense growth limits visibility to about 55 yards (50 meters). The combination of heat and moisture make Undead in this environment the most water-heavy and diseased of any you will find on the planet. When cut, bludgeoned, or shot, these zombies tend to projectiley squirt rather than ooze. Avoid combat if possible. Jungle or rain forest combat is the messiest of all Undead combat and poses a high risk of infection.

SECONDARY JUNGLES
4-21. Secondary jungle is very similar to rain forest. Prolific growth, where sunlight penetrates to the jungle floor, typifies this type of forest. Such growth happens mainly along riverbanks, on jungle fringes, and where Soldiers have cleared rain forested areas, or paths where the Undead have trod. When abandoned, tangled masses of vegetation quickly reclaim these cultivated areas. You can often find cultivated food plants among secondary jungles.

Note: Zombies in the secondary jungles described in sections 4-22 through 4-25 tend to be healthier, less water-heavy versions of their rain forest cousins. Slight weather variations and seepage of prolific nutrient-rich water into their bodies tends to enrich them.

SEMI-EVERGREEN SEASONAL AND MONSOON FORESTS
4-22. The characteristics of the American and African semi-evergreen seasonal forests correspond with those of the Asian monsoon forests:
- Their trees fall into two stories of tree strata.
    - —Upper story 60 to 79 feet (18 to 24 meters)
    - —Lower story 23 to 43 feet (7 to 13 meters)
- The diameter of the trees averages 2 feet (0.5 meter).
- Their leaves fall during a seasonal drought.

4-23. Except for the sago, nipa, and coconut palms, the same edible plants grow in these areas as in the tropical rain forests.

TROPICAL SCRUB AND THORN FORESTS
4-24. Tropical scrub and thorn forests exist on the West coast of Mexico, on the Yucatan peninsula, in Venezuela, and in Brazil; on the Northwest coast and central parts of Africa; and (in Asia) in Turkistan and India. Food plants are scarce during the dry season, and more abundant during the rainy season. The chief characteristics of tropical scrub and thorn forests include:

- They have a definite dry season.
- Trees are leafless during the dry season.
- Ground is bare, except for a few tufted plants in bunches
- Grasses are uncommon.
- Plants with thorns predominate.
- Fires occur frequently.

TROPICAL SAVANNAS

4-25. South American savannas occur in parts of Venezuela, Brazil, and Guyana. In Africa, they occur in the southern Sahara (North central Cameroon and Gabon, and Southern Sudan); Benin; Togo; most of Nigeria; the Northeastern Republic of Congo; Northern Uganda; Western Kenya; and parts of Malawi and Tanzania, Southern Zimbabwe, Mozambique, and Western Madagascar. A savanna generally:

- Exists in the tropical zones of South America and Africa.
- Looks like a broad, grassy meadow, with trees spaced at wide intervals.
- Has lots of red soil.
- Grows scattered, stunted, and gnarled trees (like apple trees) as well as palm trees.

SALTWATER SWAMPS

4-26. Saltwater swamps are common in coastal areas subject to tidal flooding. Mangrove trees thrive in these swamps, and can grow to 39 feet (12 meters). In saltwater swamps, visibility is poor, and while movement is extremely difficult for the Living, zombies here can comfortably navigate this terrain unless they are forced to swim. Sometimes, raftable streams form channels, but foot travel is usually required. Tides in saltwater swamps can vary as much as 3 feet (0.9 meter). Advice for this terrain is, try to avoid the leeches, the various insects, including no-see-ums, and crocodiles and caimans. If you can, avoid saltwater swamps. However, if they have suitable water channels, you might be able to traverse them by raft, canoe, or rubber boat.

Note: Zombies do not swim well, but reportedly have chased rafts into the water, pulled up over the sides, or bitten through the raft's rubber. Water is not a safety zone with swamp zombies.

FRESHWATER SWAMPS

4-27. Freshwater swamps exist in some low-lying inland areas. They have masses of thorny undergrowth, reeds, grasses, and occasional short palms. These all reduce visibility and make travel difficult. Freshwater swamps are dotted with large and small islands, allowing you to get out of the water. Wildlife is abundant in freshwater swamps. While not producing particularly strong or hearty zombies, damp air and stagnant water create the most foul-smelling zombies anywhere. Even by Undead standards, freshwater zombies smell wretched.

PREPARATION

4-28. Success in the jungle depends on your level of applicable knowledge and preparation.

TRAVEL THROUGH JUNGLE AREAS

4-29. With practice, you can move through thick undergrowth and jungle efficiently. Always wear long sleeves to avoid cuts and scratches.

Note: Look at a fallen zombie's exposed arm some time: it will be covered with such afflictions.

"Jungle Eye"

4-30. To move easily, you must develop a "jungle eye." That is, look through the natural breaks in foliage rather than at the foliage itself. Stoop down occasionally to look along the jungle floor.

Game Trails

4-31. You may find zombie trails you can follow. Stay alert and move slowly and steadily through dense forest or jungle. Stop periodically to listen for droning and reorient on your objective. Many jungle and forest animals follow zombie trails. These trails wind and cross, but frequently lead to water or clearings. Use these trails if they lead in your desired direction of travel.

Machete
4-32. A machete is handy against the Undead (a great decapitation weapon) and can cut through dense vegetation. Avoid cutting too much, for you will tire quickly. If using a machete, stroke upward when cutting vines to reduce noise, because sound carries long distances in the jungle.

Stick
4-33. Use a stick to part the vegetation and to help dislodge biting ants, spiders, or snakes. Never grasp brush or vines when climbing slopes, because they may have irritating spines, sharp thorns, biting insects, and snakes.

Power and Telephone Lines
4-34. In many countries, electric and telephone lines run for miles through sparsely inhabited areas. Usually, the right-of-way is clear enough to allow easy travel. When traveling along these lines, be careful as you approach a transformer and relay stations, which the Undead have entered on occasion.

WATER PROCUREMENT
4-35. Although water is abundant in most tropical environments, you may have trouble finding it, and when you do, it may not be safe to drink. Vines, roots, palm trees, and condensation are a few of the many sources of water. You can follow animals to water. Often you can get nearly clear water from muddy streams or lakes by digging a hole in sandy soil about 3 feet (1 meter) from the bank. Water will then seep into the hole. You must purify any water you get this way.

POISONOUS PLANTS
4-36. The proportion of poisonous plants in tropical regions is no greater than in any other area of the world. However, it may appear that most plants in the tropics are poisonous, due to preconceived notions and the density of plant growth in some tropical areas.

SECTION III. ARCTIC

Cold regions include arctic and subarctic areas, and areas immediately adjoining them. About 48 percent of the Northern hemisphere's total land mass is a cold region, due to the influence and range of air temperatures. Ocean currents affect cold weather and cause large areas normally included in the temperate zone to fall within the cold regions during winter periods. Elevation also has a marked effect on defining cold regions. You may face two types of cold weather environments—wet or dry. Knowing which environment your area of operation (AO) falls in will affect planning and execution. While zombies are scarcer in the arctic, they are not extinct here. Undead activity has spiked in sub- and artic regions such as Russia and Alaska, in part due to political capitulation to polluting mining companies in these regions. Grounded industrial chemicals as well as disturbed burial grounds of native people always produce a rise in Undead activity. Simply put, forever seeking flesh and brains, the Undead are found wherever there are corpses that can be reanimated and wherever the Living are found. Even the arctic.

TYPES

4-37. The two types of arctic climates are wet-cold and dry-cold.

WET-COLD WEATHER ENVIRONMENTS
4-38. Wet-cold weather conditions exist when the average temperature in a 24-hour period is 14° F (-10° C) *or above*. Characteristics of this condition include freezing temperatures at night and slightly warmer temperatures during the day. Although temperatures in a wet-cold environment are warmer than those in a dry-cold environment, the terrain is usually very sloppy due to slush and mud. Protect yourself from the wet ground, freezing rain, and wet snow. Again, wherever there is moisture, zombies will pick up ice and mud and as a result smell foul. Where sight is poor or it's hard to hear their droning, a zombie's stench will often give its location away. The icy fingers and breath of the Undead are made worse in a wet-cold environment.

DRY-COLD WEATHER ENVIRONMENTS

4-39. Dry-cold weather conditions exist when the average temperature in a 24-hour period remains *below* 14° F (-10° C). Even though these temperatures are much lower than normal, you can avoid freezing and thawing. In temperatures down to -76° F (-60° C), wear extra layers of inner clothing. Wind and low temperatures are an extremely hazardous combination.

PREPARATION

4-40. Success in the arctic begins with preparedness.

WIND CHILL

4-41. Wind chill increases the hazards in cold regions. It is the effect of moving air on exposed flesh. For example, with a 15 knot (27.8 kmph) wind and a temperature of -14° F (-10° C), the equivalent wind chill temperature is -9° F (-23 degrees C). Remember, even when no wind is blowing, your own movement, such as during skiing, running, creates "apparent" wind, will create the equivalent wind by skiing, running, being towed on skis behind a vehicle, or working around aircraft that produce windblasts.

Note: Because their skin is dead, like bark on a tree, the Undead are insensitive to temperature. Places you may find inhospitable are like any other place to a zombie. Cold weather slows and weakens the Living, but does not do this to the Undead.

TRAVEL

4-42. Soldiers will find it almost impossible to travel in deep snow without snowshoes or skis. Traveling by foot leaves a well-marked trail for pursuers to follow. If you must travel in deep snow, avoid snow-covered streams. The snow, which acts as an insulator, may have prevented ice from forming over the water. In hilly terrain, avoid areas where avalanches appear possible. On ridges, snow gathers on the lee side in overhanging piles called cornices. These often extend far out from the ridge and may break loose if stepped on.

WATER

4-43. Many sources of water exist in the arctic and subarctic. Water sources in arctic and subarctic regions are more sanitary than in other regions due to the climatic and environmental conditions. However, always purify water before drinking it. During the summer months, the best natural sources of water are freshwater lakes, streams, ponds, rivers, and springs untouched by the Undead. Water from ponds or lakes may be slightly stagnant but still usable. Running water in streams, rivers, and bubbling springs is usually fresh and suitable for drinking.

CHAPTER 5

COVER, CONCEALMENT, AND CAMOUFLAGE

If the Undead enemy can see you and you are within arm, club, or stone range, he can engage and possibly kill you. So, you must be concealed from Undead observation and have cover from Undead engagement. When the terrain does not provide natural cover and concealment, you must prepare your cover and use natural and man-made materials to camouflage yourself, your equipment, and your position. This chapter provides guidance on the preparation and use of cover, concealment, and camouflage, except for fighting positions, which are covered in Chapter 6.

SECTION I. COVER

Cover, made of natural or man-made materials, gives protection from the masses of lunging Undead and Undead observation (Figure 5-1).

Figure 5-1. Natural cover.

NATURAL COVER

5-1. Natural cover includes logs, trees, stumps, rocks, and ravines; whereas, man-made cover includes fighting positions, trenches, walls, rubble, and craters. To get protection from Undead reach in the offense or when moving, use routes that put cover between you and the Undead. For example, use ravines, gullies, hills, wooded areas, walls, and any other cover that will keep the Undead from seeing and lunging at you (Figure 5-2). Avoid open areas. Never skyline yourself on a hilltop or ridge. Any cover—even the smallest depression or fold in the ground—can help protect you from direct and indirect zombie attack.

Figure 5-2. Cover along a wall.

MAN-MADE COVER

5-2. Man-made cover includes fighting positions and protective equipment.

FIGHTING POSITION
5-3. See Chapter 6 for a detailed discussion of fighting positions (Figure 5-3).

Figure 5-3. Man-made cover.

PROTECTIVE EQUIPMENT

5-4. Man-made cover can also be an article of protective equipment that can be worn such as body armor and helmet (Figure 5-4). Body armor is protective equipment that works as a form of armor to minimize injury from scratches and—much worse—bites. The interceptor body armor (IBA) system has an outer tactical vest (OTV) which is lined with finely woven Kevlar that will stop the Undead's 9-mm yellow teeth. It also has removable neck, throat, shoulder, and groin protection—all favored striking points of the Undead. Two small-arms protective inserts may also be added to the front and back of the vest, with each plate designed to stop nails or teeth. The plates are constructed of boron carbide ceramic with a shield backing that

Figure 5-4. Body armor and helmet.

breaks down nails, teeth, and projectiles and halts their momentum. The vest also meets stringent performance specifications related to flexibility and heat stress requirements. The advanced combat helmet (ACH) provides protection against fragmentation, bullets, and blunt objects, as well as heat, flame, nails, and teeth in a balanced and stable configuration.

SIMPLIFIED COLLECTIVE PROTECTION EQUIPMENT

5-5. The M20 simplified collective protection equipment (SCPE) is an inflatable shelter that provides cover against chemical/biological warfare agents and radioactive particles (Figure 5-5), but is not advised for protection from the punching, clawing, biting, and clubbing of the Undead. However, the SCPE does provide a clean-air environment in a structure where you can perform your duties, without wearing individual protective equipment. Certain types of zombies reanimated by radioactive chemicals will carry traces of radioactivity, and the SCPE will allow you to perform administrative and communications work without fear of contamination.

Figure 5-5. Protective cover against chemical/biological warfare agents.

SECTION II. CONCEALMENT

Concealment is anything that hides you from Undead observation (Figure 5-6). Concealment does not protect you from Undead contact. Do not think that you are protected from the Undead's reach just because you are concealed. Concealment, like cover, can also be natural or manmade. (Chapter 6 discusses techniques for concealing fighting positions.)

Figure 5-6. Concealment.

NATURAL CONCEALMENT

5-6. Natural concealment includes bushes, grass, and shadows. If possible, natural concealment should not be disturbed. Man-made concealment includes Zombie Combat Uniforms (ZCUs), camouflage nets, face paint, and natural materials that have been moved from their original location. Man-made concealment must blend into natural concealment provided by the terrain.

ACTIONS AS CONCEALMENT

5-7. Light, noise, and movement discipline, and the use of camouflage, contributes to concealment. While they possess little strength and agility, zombies do have the power of sight and thus light discipline is key. This means controlling the use of lights at night by such things as not smoking in the open, not walking around with a flashlight on, and not using vehicle headlights. Noise discipline is taking action to deflect sounds generated by your unit (such as operating equipment) away from the Undead and, when possible, using methods to communicate that do not generate sounds (arm-and-hand signals). Movement discipline includes not moving about fighting positions unless necessary and not moving on routes that lack cover and concealment. In the defense, build a well-camouflaged fighting position and avoid moving about. In the offense, conceal yourself and your equipment with camouflage, and move in woods or on terrain that gives concealment. Darkness cannot hide you from Undead enemy observation in either offense or defense situations. The enemy's zombie vision allows them to find you in both daylight and darkness.

SECTION III. CAMOUFLAGE

Camouflage is anything you use to keep yourself, your equipment, and your position from being identified. Both natural and man-made material can be used for camouflage. Change and improve your camouflage often. The time between changes and improvements depends on the weather and on the material used. Natural camouflage will often die, fade, or otherwise lose its effectiveness. Likewise, man-made camouflage may wear off or fade and, as a result, Soldiers, their equipment, and their positions may stand out from their surroundings. To make it difficult for the Undead enemy to spot them, Soldiers should remember the following when using or wearing camouflage. (Chapter 6 discusses techniques for camouflaging fighting positions.):

MOVEMENT

5-8. Zombies respond to movement and activity. When you give arm-and-hand signals or walk about your position, your movement can be seen by the naked eye at long ranges. In the defense, stay low. Move only when necessary. In the offense, move only on covered and concealed routes.

POSITIONS

5-9. Avoid putting anything where the Undead expects to find it, like a farmhouse, parked car, or shed out back. Build positions on the side of a hill, away from road junctions or lone buildings, and in covered and concealed places. Avoid open areas, especially fields and cemeteries.

OUTLINES AND SHADOWS

5-10. These can reveal your position or equipment to an Undead observer. Break up outlines and shadows with camouflage. When moving, try to stay in the shadows.

SHINE

5-11. Anything shiny will naturally attract the Undead's attention. In the dark, a burning cigarette or flashlight will give you away. In daylight, reflected light from any polished surface such as shiny mess gear; a worn helmet; wallet photograph of mother, father, boyfriend, girlfriend, wife, or husband; a watch crystal and band, or exposed skin will do it. Any light, or reflection of light, can help the Undead detect your position. To reduce shine, cover your skin with clothing and face paint. Dull equipment and vehicle surfaces with paint, mud, or other camouflaging material or substance.

WARNING

In a nuclear attack, during which zombie uprisings are highly likely, darkly painted skin can absorb more thermal energy and may burn more readily than bare skin. Burnt skin may make your appearance look like that of a zombie, thereby increasing the chances of friendly fire casualty.

SHAPE

5-12. Certain shapes, such as an exposed head (housing the Undead's favorite source of nourishment, the brain) or the silhouette of a young woman, are easily recognizable to the Undead. Camouflage, conceal, and break up familiar shapes to make them blend in with their surroundings, but avoid overdoing it.

COLORS

5-13. If your skin, uniform, or equipment colors stand out against the background, the Undead can detect you more easily than he could otherwise. For example, ZCUs stand out against a backdrop of snow-covered terrain. Once again, camouflage yourself and your equipment to blend with the surroundings (Figure 5-7).

DISPERSION

5-14. This means spreading heroic Soldiers, cowardly Soldiers, and attractive female Soldiers over a wide area. For example the Undead enemy can detect a bunch of teenaged Soldiers more easily than they can detect a lone teen. Spread out. Unit SOP or unit leaders vary distances between you and your fellow Soldiers depending on the terrain, degree of visibility, and Undead situation.

Figure 5-7. Soldier in arctic camouflage.

Figure 5-8. Camouflaged soldiers.

PREPARATION

5-15. Before camouflaging, study the terrain and vegetation of the area in which you are operating. Next, pick and use the camouflage material that best blends with the area (Figures 5-8). When moving from one area to another, change camouflage as needed to blend with the surroundings. Take grass, leaves, brush, and other material from your location and apply it to your uniform and equipment, and put face paint on your skin.

INDIVIDUAL TECHNIQUES

HELMET

5-16. A zombie's first point of attack is the head, housing the brain. Spotting a moving head, a zombie is likely to call out "brains!" thereby attracting fellow zombies. Thus, covering the helmet is important. Camouflage your helmet with the issue helmet cover or make a cover of cloth or burlap that is colored to blend with the terrain (Figure 5-9). Leaves, grass, or sticks can also be attached to the cover. Use

Figure 5-9. Camouflaged helmet.

camouflage bands, strings, burlap strips, or rubber bands to hold those in place. If you have no material for a helmet cover, disguise and dull helmet surface with irregular patterns of paint or mud.

UNIFORM

5-17. It may be necessary to add more camouflage to blend better with the surroundings. To do this, put mud on your outfit or attach leaves, grass, or small branches to it. Too much camouflage, however, may draw attention. When operating on snow-covered ground wear overwhites (if issued) to help blend with the snow. If overwhites are not issued, use white cloth, such as white bed sheets, to get the same effect. While zombies are not afraid of sunlight and are immune to cold temperatures, they're rarely seen in the snow and if you see one, it is probably lost.

SKIN

5-18. Exposed skin reflects light and may draw a zombie's attention. Even very dark skin, because of its natural oil, will reflect light. The advanced camouflage face paint in compact form comes both with and without insect repellent. The active ingredient of the repellant is N, N-diethyl-meta-toluamide (commonly known as DEET). The camouflage face paint provides visual and near-IR camouflage protection. The version with DEET also repels insects for eight hours. Zombies never attract bugs, though they do stink. So, they will be attracted to insect swarms, where there is likely a Living human. In zombie combat, it is recommended that Soldiers use the face paint with the insect repellent. Both face-paint compacts contain five compartments of pigmented formulations (jungle, snow, sand, night, and rotting flesh). The compacts provide sufficient material for 20 applications of jungle, snow, and sand, and 10 applications of night and rotting flesh. The compact is suitable for multi-terrain environmental conditions from arctic to desert. Face paints with insect repellent are supplied in a tan colored compact, while the non-repellent face paints are furnished in an olive drab compact for quick identification (Figure 5-10). When applying camouflage to your skin, work with a buddy (in pairs) and help each other. Apply a two-color combination of camouflage pigment in an irregular pattern. Do not apply camouflage paint if there is a chance of frostbite. The pigment may prevent other Soldiers from recognizing the whitish discoloration, the first symptoms of the skin freezing.

WARNING

Only use rotting flesh pigment when in an evasion scenario when fellow Soldiers are not in the vicinity. Rotting flesh pigment will help you blend in with and therefore escape the Undead enemy, but it will also make you a target for your own units.

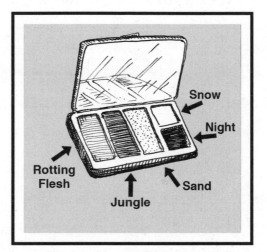

Figure 5-10. Advanced camouflage face paint.

Note: If you can acquire a yellow pigment—from a packet of mustard, for example—you can match your teeth and nails to those of the Undead.

5-19. Paint shiny areas (forehead, cheekbones, nose, ears, and chin) with a dark color. Paint shadow areas (around the eyes, under the nose, and under the chin) with a light color. In addition to the face, paint the exposed skin on the back of the neck, arms, and hands. Palms of hands are not normally camouflaged if arm-and-hand signals are to be used. Remove all jewelry to further reduce shine or reflection. When camouflage sticks/compacts are not issued, use burnt torch, bark, charcoal, lamp black, or light-colored mud (Table 5-1).

Table 5-1. Application of camouflage face paint to skin.

CAMOUFLAGE MATERIAL	SKIN COLOR	SHINE AREAS	SHADOW AREAS
	Light or Dark	Forehead, Cheekbones, Ears, Nose, and Chin	Around Eyes, Under Nose, and Under Chin
Snow and Light Green Stick	All Troops Use in Areas with Green Vegetation	Use Snow	Use Light Green
Sand and Light Green Stick	All Troops Use in Areas Lacking Green Vegetation	Use Light Green	Use Sand
Snow	All Troops Use Only in Snow-Covered Terrain	Use Snow	Use Snow
Rotting Flesh	All Troops Use Only When Isolated Among the Undead	Rotting Flesh	Rotting Flesh
Burnt Cork, Bark Charcoal, or Lamp Black	All Troops, If Camouflage Sticks Not Available	Use	Do Not Use
Light-Color Mud	All Troops, If Camouflage Sticks Not Available	Do Not Use	Use

CHAPTER 6

FIGHTING POSITIONS

Whether your unit is in a defensive perimeter or on an ambush line, you must seek cover from attacks, and concealment from observation. From the time you prepare and occupy a fighting position, you should continue to improve it. How far you get depends on how much time you have, regardless of whether it is a hasty position or a well-prepared one with overhead cover (OHC). This chapter discusses:

- Cover and concealment.
- Sectors and fields of fire.
- Hasty and deliberate fighting positions.

COVER

6-1. To get this protection in the defense, build a fighting position to add to the natural cover afforded by the terrain (Figure 6-1). The cover of your fighting position will protect you from heaved rocks and friendly fire fragments, and place a greater thickness of shielding material or earth between you and the blast wave of nuclear reactors or a meteorite's radiation, two scenarios during which zombies are likely.

6-2. Three different types of cover—overhead, frontal, and flank/rear cover—are used to make fighting positions. In addition, positions can be connected by tunnels and trenches. These allow Soldiers to move between positions for engagements or resupply, while remaining protected. (Chapter 5 discussed cover in general.)

Figure 6-1. Man-made cover.

OVERHEAD COVER

6-3. Your completed position should have OHC, which enhances survivability by protecting you from indirect fire and fragmentation.

FRONTAL COVER

6-4. Your position needs frontal cover to protect you from crude projectiles to the front. Frontal cover allows you to fire to the oblique, as well as to hide your muzzle flash.

FLANK AND REAR COVER

6-5. When used with frontal and overhead cover, flank and rear cover protects you from direct Undead attack and friendly fire (Figure 6-2). Natural frontal cover such as rocks, trees, logs, and rubble is best, because it is hard for the Undead to detect. When natural cover is unavailable, use the dirt you remove to construct the fighting position. You can improve the effectiveness of dirt as a cover by putting it in sandbags. Fill them only three-quarters full.

Figure 6-2. Cover.

CONCEALMENT

6-6. If your position can be detected, it can be hit by the Undead. Therefore, your position must be so well hidden that the Undead will have a hard time detecting it, even after he reaches stone-heaving range. (Chapter 5 discussed cover in general.)

NATURAL, UNDISTURBED MATERIALS

6-7. Natural, undisturbed concealment is better than man-made concealment. While digging your position, try not to disturb the natural concealment around it. Put the unused dirt from the hole behind the position and camouflage it. Camouflage material that does not have to be replaced (rocks, logs, live bushes, and grass) is best. Natural, undisturbed concealment materials:

- Are already prepared.
- Seldom attract Undead attention.
- Need no replacement.

MAN-MADE CONCEALMENT

6-8. Your position must be concealed from aircraft as well as from the Undead on the ground. If the position is under a bush or tree, or in a building, it is less visible from above. Spread leaves, straw, or grass on the floor of the hole to keep freshly dug earth from contrasting with the ground around it. Man-made concealment must blend with its surroundings so that it cannot be detected, and must be replaced if it changes color or dries out.

Note: *Though never documented, there have been reports of the Living turning Undead on certain airline flights, such as the infamous Flight 103 containing a number of men and women from the Love Canal area in Western New York in 1978.*

CAMOUFLAGE

6-9. When building a fighting position, camouflage it and the dirt taken from it. Camouflage the dirt used as frontal, flank, rear, and overhead cover (OHC). Also, camouflage the bottom of the hole to prevent detection from the air. If necessary, take excess dirt away from the position (to the rear).

- Too much camouflage material may actually disclose a position. Get your camouflage material from a wide area. An area stripped of all or most of its vegetation may draw attention. Do not wait until the position is complete to camouflage it. Camouflage the position as you build.
- Hide mirrors, food containers, and white underpants and towels. Do not remove your shirt in the open. Your skin may shine and be seen. Never use fires where there is a chance that the flame will be seen or the smoke will be smelled by the Undead. Also, cover up tracks and other signs of movement. When camouflage is complete, inspect the position from the Undead's side.

SECTORS AND FIELDS OF FIRE

6-10. Although a fighting position should provide maximum protection for you and your equipment, the primary consideration is always given to sectors of fire and effective weapons employment. Weapons systems are sited where natural or existing positions are available, or where terrain will provide the most protection while maintaining the ability to engage the Undead. You should always consider how best to use available terrain, and how you can modify it to provide the best sectors of fire, while maximizing the capabilities of your weapon system.

SECTOR OF FIRE

6-11. A sector of fire is the area into which you must observe and fire. When your leader assigns you a fighting position, he should also assign you a primary and secondary sector of fire. The primary sector of fire is to the oblique of your position, and the secondary sector of fire is to the front.

FIELD OF FIRE

6-12. To be able to see and fire into your sectors of fire, you might have to "clear a field" of vegetation and other obstructions. Fields of fire are within the range of your weapons. A field of fire to the oblique lets you hit the attackers from an unexpected angle. It also lets you support the positions next to you. When you fire to the oblique, your fire interlocks with that of other positions, creating a wall of fire that the Undead must pass through. When clearing a field of fire:

- Avoid disclosing your position by careless or excessive clearing.
- Leave a thin, natural screen of vegetation to hide your position.
- In sparsely wooded areas, cut off lower branches of large, scattered trees.
- Clear underbrush only where it blocks your view.
- Remove cut brush, limbs, and weeds so the Undead will not spot them.
- Cover cuts on trees and bushes forward of your position with mud, dirt, or snow.
- Leave no trails as clues for the Undead.

HASTY AND DELIBERATE FIGHTING POSITIONS

6-13. The two types of fighting positions are hasty and deliberate. Which you construct depends on time and equipment available, and the required level of protection. Fighting positions are designed and constructed to protect you and your weapon system.

HASTY FIGHTING POSITION

6-14. Hasty fighting positions, used when there is little time for preparation, should be behind whatever cover is available. However, the term hasty does not mean that there is no digging. If a natural hole or ditch is available, use it. This position should give frontal cover from objects lobbed by the Undead but allow firing to the front and the oblique. Any crater 2 to 3 feet (0.61 to 1 meter) wide, offers immediate cover (except for overhead) and concealment. Digging a steep face on the side toward the Undead creates a hasty fighting position. A skirmisher's trench is a shallow position that provides a hasty prone fighting position. When you need immediate shelter from Undead attack, and there are no defilade firing positions available, lie prone or on your side, scrape the soil with an entrenching tool, and pile the soil in a low parapet between yourself and the Undead. In all but the hardest ground, you can use this technique to quickly form a shallow, body-length pit. Orient the trench so it is oblique to the Undead. This keeps your silhouette low, and offers some protection from heaved objects.

6-15. The prone position is a further refinement of the skirmisher's trench. It serves as a good firing position and provides you with better protection against the direct hurled objects than the crater position or the skirmisher's trench. The hole should be about 18 inches (46 centimeters) deep and use the dirt from the hole to build cover around the edge of the position (Figure 6-3).

DELIBERATE FIGHTING POSITION

6-16. Deliberate fighting positions are modified hasty positions prepared during periods of relaxed Undead pressure. Your leader will assign the sectors of fire for your position's weapon system before preparation

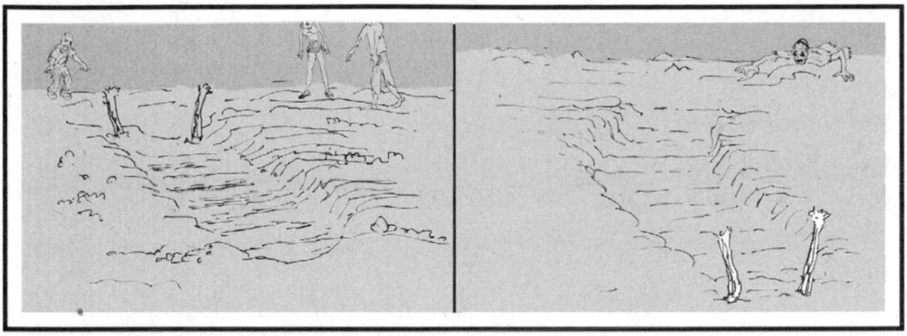

Figure 6-3. Prone position (hasty).

begins. Small holes are dug for automatic rifle bipod legs, so the rifle is as close to ground level as possible. Continued improvements are made to strengthen the position during the period of occupation. Improvements include adding OHC, digging grenade sumps (explained later), adding trenches to adjacent positions, and maintaining camouflage.

TWO-MAN FIGHTING POSITION

6-17. Prepare a two-man position in four stages. Your leader must inspect the position at each stage before you may move to the next stage (Table 6-1).

Table 6-1. Construction of two-man fighting position.

Parapets	Overhead Cover

Enable you to engage the Undead within your assigned sector of fire.
 	
Provide you with protection from directly hurled objects (sticks, heads, cats). Construct parapets—
 	
    Thickness: Minimum 39 in (1m) (length of M16 rifle)
    Height: 10 to 12 inches (25 to 30 centimeters) (length of a bayonet) to the front, flank, and rear.
	Protects you from indirectly hurled objects. Your leaders will identify requirements for additional OHC based on threat capabilities.
	
	    Thickness: Minimum 18 inches (46 cm) (length of open entrenching tool)
	    Concealment: Use enough to make your position undetectable.

Overhead Cover

6-18. Overhead cover may be built up or down.

Built-Up Overhead Cover

6-19. Built-up OHC has cover that is built up to 18 inches (46 centimeters) to maximize protection/cover of the fighting position.

Stage 1

6-20. Establish sectors and decide whether to build OHC up or down. Your fearless leaders must consider the factors of the mission, enemy, terrain, troops and equipment, time available, and civil considerations (METT-TC) in order to make a decision on the most appropriate fighting position to construct. For example due to more open terrain your leader may decide to use built-down OHC (Figure 6-4 and Figure 6-5):

1. Check fields of fire from the prone position.
2. Assign sector of fire (primary and secondary).
3. Emplace sector stakes (right and left) to define your sectors of fire. Sector stakes prevent accidental firing into friendly positions. Items such as tent poles, metal pickets, wooden stakes, oars, tree branches, or sandbags will all make good sector stakes. The sector stakes must be sturdy and stick out of the ground at least 18 inches (46 centimeters); this will prevent your weapon from being pointed out of your sector.
4. Emplace aiming and limiting stakes to help you fire into dangerous approaches at night and at other times when visibility is poor. Forked tree limbs about 12 inches (30 centimeters) long make good stakes. Put one stake (possibly sandbags) near the edge of the hole to rest the stock of your rifle on. Then put another stake forward of the rear (first) stake/sandbag toward each dangerous approach. The forward stakes are used to hold the rifle barrel.
5. Emplace grazing fire logs or sandbags to achieve grazing fire 1 meter above ground level.
6. Decide whether to build OHC up or down, based on potential Undead observation of position.

7. Scoop out elbow holes to keep your elbows from moving around when you fire.
8. Trace position outline.
9. Clear primary and secondary fields of fire.

Note: Keep in mind that the widths of all the fighting positions are only an approximate distance. This is due to the individual Soldier's equipment such as the IBA and the modular lightweight load-carrying equipment.

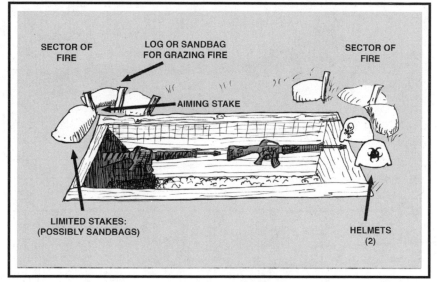

Figure 6-4. Establishment of sectors and building method.

Stage 2

6-21. Place supports for OHC stringers and construct parapet retaining walls (Figure 6-6 and Figure 6-7):
1. Emplace OHC supports to front and rear of position.
2. Ensure you have at least 12 inches (30 centimeters), which is about 1-helmet length distance from the edge of the hole to the beginning of the supports needed for the OHC.
3. If you plan to use logs or cut timber, secure them in place with strong stakes from 2 to 3 inches (5 to 7 centimeters) in diameter and 18 inches (46 centimeters) long. Short U-shaped pickets will work.

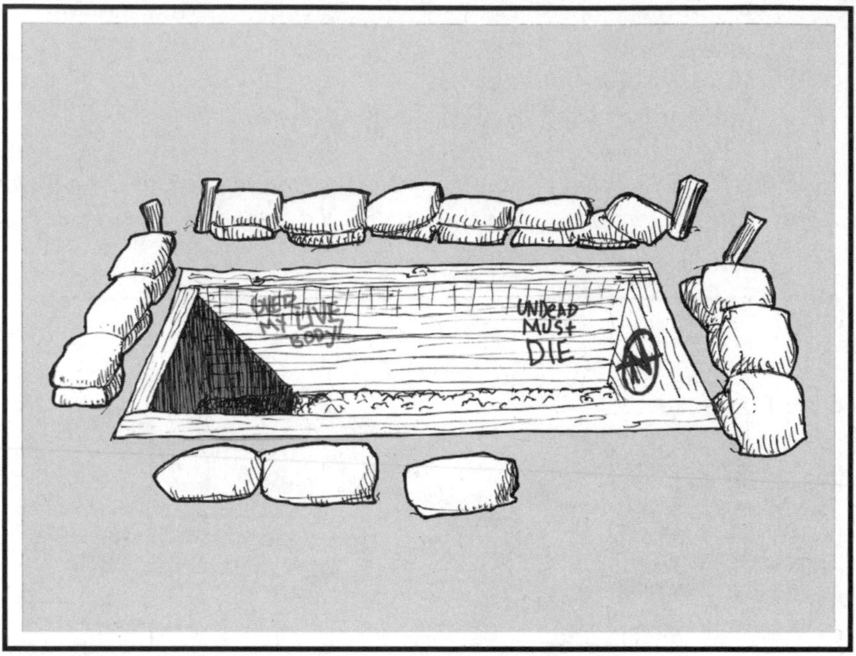

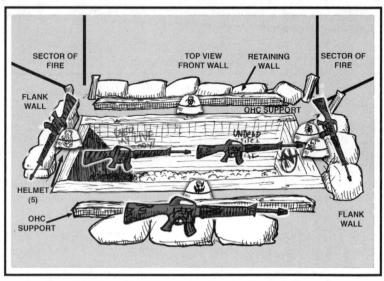

Figure 6-5. Two-man fighting position (Stage 1).

SECTOR OF
FIRE

TOP VIEW
FRONT WALL

RETAINING
WALL

SECTOR OF
FIRE

FLANK
WALL

OHC SUPPORT

HELMET
(5)

OHC
SUPPORT

FLANK
WALL

Figure 6-6. Placement of OHC supports and construction of retaining walls.

4. Dig in about half the height.
   a. Front retaining wall—At least 10 inches (25 centimeters) high, (two filled sandbags) deep, and two M16s long.
   b. Rear retaining wall—At least 10 inches (25 centimeters) high, and one M16 long.
   c. Flank retaining walls—At least 10 inches (25 centimeters) high, and one M16 long.
5. Start digging hole; use soil to fill sandbags for walls.

Figure 6-7. Two-man fighting position (Stage 2).

Stage 3

6-22. Dig position and place stringers for OHC (Figure 6-8, Figure 6-9, and Figure 6-10):

1. Ensure maximum depth is armpit deep (if soil conditions permit).
2. Use spoil from hole to fill parapets in the order of front, flanks, and rear.
3. Dig walls vertically.
4. If site soil properties cause unstable soil conditions, construct revetments (Figure 6-11) and consider sloping walls.

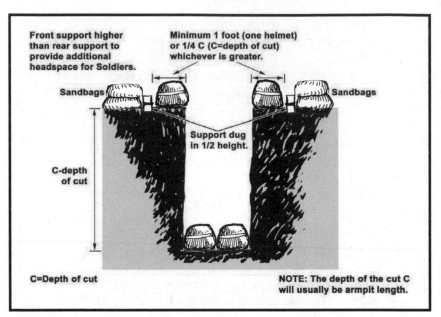

Figure 6-8. Digging of position (side view).

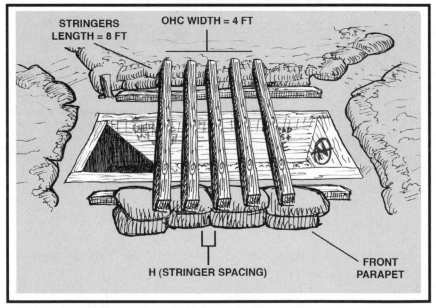

Figure 6-9. Placement of stringers for OHC.

Figure 6-10. Two-man fighting position (Stage 3).

Figure 6-11. Revetment construction.

5. For sloped walls, first dig a vertical hole, and then slope walls at 1:4 ratio (move 12 inches [30 centimeters] horizontally for each 4 feet [1.22 meters] vertically).

6. Dig two grenade sumps in the floor (one on each end). If a member of the Undead throws a grenade into the hole, kick or throw it into one of the sumps. The sump will absorb most of the blast. The rest of the blast will be directed straight up and out of the hole. Dig the grenade sumps as wide as the entrenching tool blade; at least as deep as an entrenching tool and as long as the position floor is wide (Figure 6-12).

Note: A commonly asked question is, Do zombies have grenades? The answer is that while the Undead lack sophisticated weaponry, they can lob a grenade back toward where it came. Unlike a human Soldier, a zombie has no fear and in fact is drawn to the metal and smoke. While some will meet their end this way, a few will return grenade fire, so it is better to be safe than sorry.

7. Dig a storage compartment in the bottom of the back wall; the size of the compartment depends on the amount of equipment and ammunition to be stored (Figure 6-13).

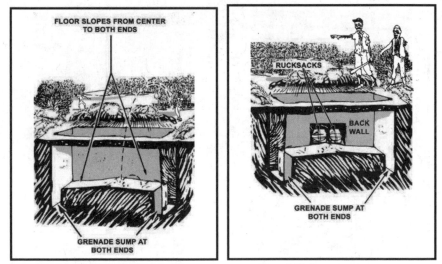

Figure 6-12. Grenade sumps.   Figure 6-13. Storage compartments.

8. Install revetments to prevent wall collapse/cave-in:
   a. Required in unstable soil conditions.
   b. Use plywood or sheeting material and pickets to revet walls.
   c. Tie back pickets and posts.
   d. Emplace OHC stringers.
   e. Use 2x4s, 4x4s, or pickets ("U" facing down).
   f. Make OHC stringers standard length, which is 8 feet (2.4 meters). This is long enough to allow sufficient length in case walls slope.
   g. Use "L" for stringer length and "H" for stringer spacing.
9. Remove the second layer of sandbags in the front and rear retaining walls to make room for the stringers. Place the same sandbags on top of the stringers once you have the stringers properly positioned.

Stage 4

6-23. Install OHC and camouflage (Figure 6-14 and Figure 6-15):
   1. Install overhead cover
   2. Use plywood, sheeting mats as a dustproof layer (could be boxes, plastic panel, or interlocked U-shaped pickets). Standard dustproof layer is 4'x4' sheets of ¾-inch plywood centered over dug position.
   3. Nail plywood dustproof layer to stringers.
   4. Use at least 18 inches (46 centimeters) of sand-filled sandbags for overhead burst protection (four layers). At a minimum, these sandbags must cover an area that extends to the sandbags used for the front and rear retaining walls.
   5. Use plastic or a poncho for waterproofing layer.
   6. Fill center cavity with soil from dug hold and surrounding soil.
   7. Use surrounding topsoil and camouflage screen systems.
   8. Use soil from hole to fill sandbags, OHC cavity, and blend in with surroundings.

Note: While you are doing the unpleasant work of securing your shelter, know that the Undead make no such preparations. Other than open graves and loose caskets, zombies have no shelters and thus exist with the rot, insects, and infection. Here the Living have an advantage.

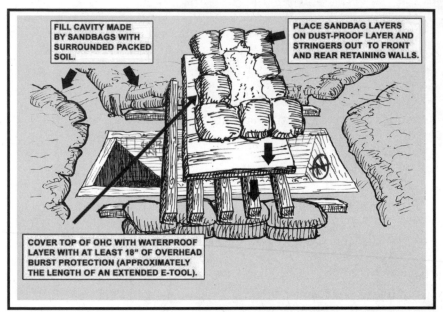

Figure 6-14. Installation of overhead cover.

Figure 6-15. Two-man fighting position with built-up OHC (Stage 4).

Built-Down Overhead Cover

6-24. This should not exceed 12 inches (30 centimeters). This lowers the profile of the fighting position, which aids in avoiding detection. Unlike a built-up OHC, a built-down OHC has the following traits (Table 6-2, Figure 6-16, and Figure 6-17):

Table 6-2. Specifications for built-down overhead cover.

Maximum 12 inches (30 centimeters) High
- You can build parapets up to 30 centimeters. Taper the overhead portions and parapets above the ground surface to conform to the natural lay of the ground.

Minimum Three M16s Long
- This gives you adequate fighting space between the end walls of the fighting position and the overhead cover. This takes 2.5 hours longer to dig in normal soil conditions.

Firing Platform for Elbows
- You must construct a firing platform in the natural terrain upon which to rest your elbows. The firing platform will allow the use of the natural ground surface as a grazing fire platform.

ONE-MAN FIGHTING POSITION

6-25. Sometimes you may have to build and occupy a one-man fighting position, for example, an ammunition bearer in a machine gun team. Except for its size, a one-man position is built the same way as a two-man fighting position. The hole of a one-man position is only large enough for you and your equipment. It does not have the security of a two-person position; therefore, it must allow a Soldier to shoot to the front or oblique from behind frontal cover.

MACHINE GUN FIGHTING POSITION

6-26. Construct fighting positions for machine guns so the gun fires to the front or oblique. However, the primary sector of fire is usually

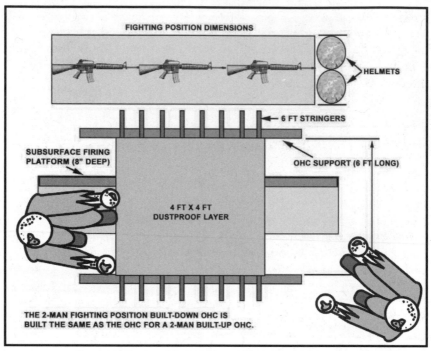

Figure 6-16. Two-man fighting position with built-down OHC (top view).

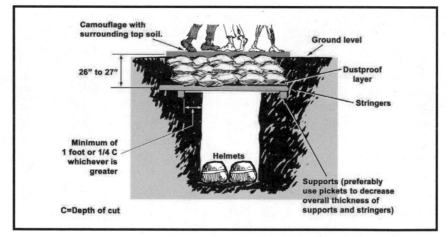

Figure 6-17. Two-man fighting position with built-down OHC (side view).

oblique so the gun can fire across your unit in front. Two Soldiers (gun slayer and assistant gun slayer) are required to operate the weapon system. Therefore, the hole is shaped so both the gunner and assistant gunner can get to the gun and fire it from either side of the frontal protection. The gun's height is reduced by digging the tripod platform down as much as possible. However, the platform is dug to keep the gun traversable across the entire sector of fire. The tripod is used on the side with the primary sector of fire, and the bipod legs are used on the side with the secondary sector. When changing from primary to secondary sectors, the machine gun is moved but the tripod stays in place. With a three-Soldier crew for a machine gun, the slug packer or loader digs a one-Soldier fighting position to the flank. From this position, the Soldier can see and shoot to the front and oblique. The ammunition bearer's position is connected to the gun position by a crawl trench so the bearer can transport ammunition or replace one of the gunners.

6-27. When a machine gun has only one sector of fire, dig only half of the position. With a three-man crew, the third Soldier (the slug packer or loader) digs a one-man fighting position. A one-man position is built the same as a two-man fighting position. The hole of a one-man position is only large enough for you and your equipment. Usually, his position is on the same side of the machine gun as its FPL (final protective line) or PDF (principal direction of fire). From that position, he can observe and fire into the machine gun's secondary sector and, at the same time, see the slayer and assistant slayer. The ammunition bearer's position is connected to the machine gun position by a crawl trench so that he can bring ammunition to the gun or replace the slayer or his assistant.

Stage 1
6-28. Establish sectors (primary and secondary) of fire, and then outline position (Figure 6-18):
1. Check fields of fire from prone.
2. Assign sector of fire (primary and secondary) and FPL or PDF.
3. Emplace aiming stakes.
4. Decide whether to build OHC up or down, based on potential Undead observation of position.

5. Trace position outline to include location of two distinct firing platforms.
6. Mark position of the tripod legs where the gun can be laid on the FPL or PDF.
7. Clear primary and secondary fields of fire.

Note: *The FPL is a line on which the gun fires grazing fire across the unit is front. Grazing fire is fired 1 meter above the ground. When an FPL is not assigned, a PDF is assigned. A PDF is a direction toward which the gun must be pointed when not firing at targets in other parts of its sector.*

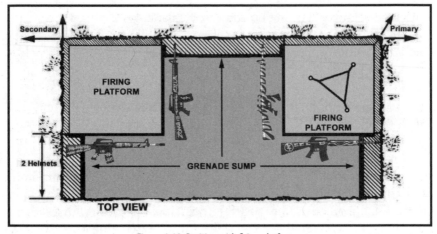

Figure 6-18. Position with firing platforms.

Stage 2

6-29. Dig firing platforms and emplace supports for OHC stringers, and then construct the parapet retaining walls:
1. Emplace OHC supports to front and rear of position.
2. Center OHC in position, and place supports as you did for Stage 2, two-man fighting position.
3. Construct the same as you did for Stage 2, two-man fighting position.
4. Dig firing platforms 6 to 8 inches (15 to 20 centimeters) deep and then position machine gun to cover primary sector of fire.
5. Use soil to fill sandbags for walls.

Stage 3

6-30. Dig position and build parapets, and then place stringers for the OHC (Figure 6-19):

1. Dig the position to a maximum armpit depth around the firing platform.
2. Use soil from hole to fill parapets in order of front, flanks, and rear.
3. Dig grenade sumps and slope floor toward them.
4. Install revetment if needed.
5. Follow same steps as for two-man fighting position.
6. Place stringers for OHC.
7. Follow same steps established for two-man fighting position.
8. Make stringers at least 8 feet (2.44 meters) long.

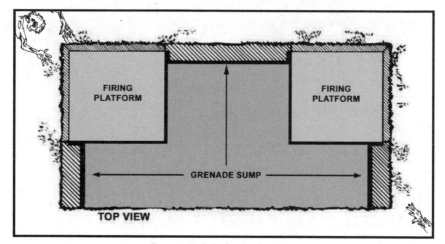

Figure 6-19. Grenade sump locations.

Stage 4

6-31. Install overhead cover (OHC) and camouflage (Figure 6-20):

1. For a machine gun position, build the OHC the same as you would for a two-man fighting position.
2. Use surrounding topsoil and camouflage screen systems.
3. Ensure no Undead observation within 115 feet (35 meters) of position.

4. Use soil from hole to fill sandbags and OHC cavity, or to spread around and blend position in with surrounding ground.

Figure 6-20. Machine gun fighting position with OHC.

CLOSE COMBAT MISSILE FIGHTING POSITIONS

6-32. The following paragraphs discuss close combat missile fighting positions for the AT4 and Javelin:

AT4 POSITION

6-33. The AT4 is fired from the fighting positions previously described. However, backblast may cause friendly casualties of Soldiers in the position's backblast area. You should ensure that any walls, parapets, large trees, or other objects to the rear will not deflect the backblast. When the AT4 is fired from a two-Soldier position, you must ensure the backblast area is clear. The front edge of a fighting position is a good elbow rest to help you steady the weapon and gain accuracy. Stability is better if your body is leaning against the position's front or side wall.

STANDARD JAVELIN FIGHTING POSITION WITH OVERHEAD COVER

6-34. The standard Javelin fighting position has cover to protect you from direct and indirect fires (Figure 6-21). The position is prepared the same as the two-man fighting position with two additional steps. First, the back wall of the position is extended and sloped rearward, which serves as storage area. Secondly, the front and side parapets are extended twice the length as the dimensions of the two-man fighting position with the javelin's primary and secondary seated firing platforms added to both sides.

Note: When a Javelin is fired, the muzzle end extends 6 inches (15 centimeters) beyond the front of the position, and the rear launcher extends out over the rear of the position. As the missile leaves the launcher, stabilizing fins unfold. You must keep the weapon at least 6 inches (15 centimeters) above the ground when firing to leave room for the fins. OHC that would allow firing from beneath it is usually built if the backblast area is clear.

RANGE CARDS

6-35. A range card, a rough plan of the terrain around a weapon position, is a sketch of the assigned sector that a direct fire weapon system is intended to cover. Range cards are prepared immediately upon arrival in a position.

COMPONENTS

6-36. A range card is comprised of the following.

Sectors of Fire—A sector of fire is an area to be covered by fire that is assigned to an individual, a weapon, or a unit. You are normally assigned a primary and secondary sector of fire. Fire into your secondary sector of fire only if your primary sector has no targets, or if ordered to do so. Your gun's primary sector includes a FPL and a PDF.

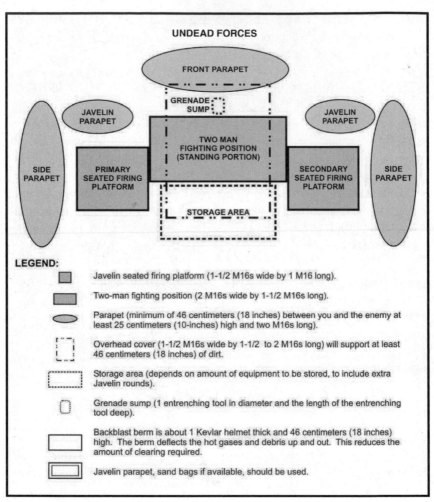

Figure 6-21. Standard Javelin fighting position.

Principal Direction of Fire—A PDF is a direction of fire assigned priority to cover an area that has good fields of fire or has a likely dismounted avenue of approach. The gun is positioned to fire directly down this approach rather than across the platoon's front. It also provides mutual support to an adjacent unit. Machine guns are sighted using the PDF if an FPL has not been assigned. If a PDF is assigned and other targets are not being engaged, machine guns remain on the PDF.

Final Protective Line—An FPL is a predetermined line along which grazing fire is placed to stop an Undead assault. Where terrain allows, your leader assigns an FPL to your weapon. An FPL becomes the machine gun's part of the unit in final protective fires. The FPL will be assigned to you only if your leader determines there is a good distance of grazing fire. If there is, the FPL will then dictate the location of the primary sector. The FPL will become the primary sector limit (right or left) closest to friendly troops. When not firing at other targets, you will lay your gun on the FPL or PDF.

Dead Space—Dead space is an area that direct fire weapons cannot hit. The area behind houses and hills, cemeteries, hospitals, power plants, large meteorite craters, within orchards or defilades for example, is dead space. The extent of grazing fire and dead space may be determined in two ways. In the preferred method, the machine gun is adjusted for elevation and direction. Your assistant gunner walks along the FPL while you aim through the sights. In places where his waist (midsection) falls below your point of aim, dead space exists.

AUTOMATIC WEAPON RANGE CARD

6-37.　To prepare this range card—
1. Orient the card so both the primary and secondary sectors of fire (if assigned) can fit on it.
2. Draw a rough sketch of the terrain to the front of your position. Include any prominent natural and man-made features that could be likely targets.
3. Draw your position at the bottom of the sketch. Do not put in the weapon symbol at this time.
4. Fill in the marginal data to include—
5. Gun number (or squad).
6. Unit (only platoon and company) and date.
7. Magnetic north arrow.
8. Use the lensatic compass to determine magnetic north; and sketch in the magnetic north arrow on the card with its base starting at the top of the marginal data section.
9. Determine the location of your gun position in relation to a prominent terrain feature, such as a hilltop, road junction, or building. Do not sketch in the gun symbol at this time.

10. Using your compass, determine the azimuth in degrees from the terrain feature to the gun position. (Compute the back azimuth from the gun to the feature by adding or subtracting 180 degrees.)
11. Determine the distance between the gun and the feature by pacing or plotting the distance on a map.
12. Sketch in the terrain feature on the card in the lower left or right hand corner (whichever is closest to its actual direction on the ground) and identify it.
13. Connect the sketch of the position and the terrain feature with a barbed line from the feature to the gun.
14. Write in the distance in meters (above the barbed line).
15. Write in the azimuth in degrees from the feature to the gun (below the barbed line).

Final Protective Fires

6-38. To add an FPL to your range card (Figure 6-22):
1. Sketch in the limits of the primary sector of fire as assigned by your leader.
2. Sketch in the FPL on your sector limit as assigned.
3. Determine dead space on the FPL by having your AG (assistant gunner) walk the FPL. Watch him walk down the line and mark spaces that cannot be grazed.
4. Sketch dead space by showing a break in the symbol for an FPL, and write in the range to the beginning and end of the dead space.
5. Label all targets in your primary sector in order of priority. The FPL is number one.

Primary Direction of Fire

6-39. To prepare your range card when assigned a PDF instead of an FPL (Figure 6-23):
1. Sketch in the limits of the primary sector of fire as assigned by your leader (sector should not exceed 875 mils).
2. Sketch in the symbol for an automatic weapon oriented on the most dangerous target within your sector (as designated

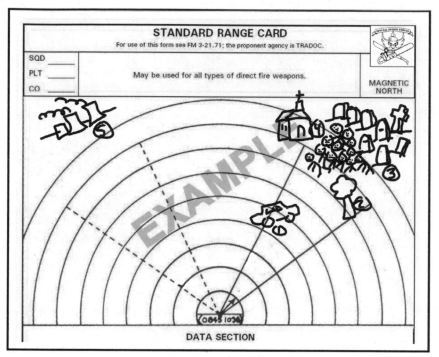

Figure 6-22. Primary sector with an FPL.

by your leader). The PDF will be target number one in your
sector. All other targets will be numbered in priority.

3. Sketch in your secondary sector of fire (as assigned) and label
targets within the secondary sector with the range in meters
from your gun to each target. Use the bipod when it is necessary to fire into your secondary sector. The secondary sector is
drawn using a broken line. Sketch in aiming stakes, if used.

Data Section

6-40. The data section (Figure 6-24) of the range card lists the data necessary to engage targets identified in the sketch. The sketch does not have to
be to scale, but the data must be accurate. The data section of the card can
be placed on the reverse side or below the sketch if there is room. (Figure
6-25 shows an example completed data section.) Draw a data section block
(if you do not have a printed card) with the following items:

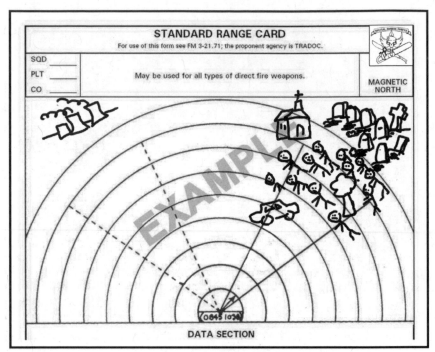

Figure 6-23. Complete sketch with PDF.

DATA SECTION

POSITION IDENTIFICATION			DATE		
WEAPON			EACH CIRCLE EQUALS METERS		
NO.	DIRECTION/ DEFLECTION	ELEVATION	RANGE	AMMO	DESCRIPTION
REMARKS:					

DA FORM 5517-R, FEB 1986

USAPA V1.01

Figure 6-24. Data section.

Prepare

1. Center the traversing hand wheel.
2. Lay the gun for direction.
3. When assigned an FPL, lock the traversing slide on the extreme left or right of the bar, depending on which side of your primary sector the FPL is on.
4. Align the barrel on the FPL by moving the tripod legs. Do not enter a direction in the data section for the FPL.
5. When assigned a PDF, align your gun on the primary sector by traversing the slide to one side and then move the tripod to align the barrel on your sector limit. Align the PDF by traversing the slide until your gun is aimed at the center of the target.
6. Fix the tripod legs in place by digging in or sandbagging them.

Read Direction to Target

1. Lay your gun on the center of the target.
2. Read the direction directly off the traversing bar at the left edge of the traversing bar slide.
3. Enter the reading under the direction column of your range card data section.
4. Determine the left or right reading based on the direction of the barrel, just the opposite of the slide.
5. Lay your gun on the base of the target by rotating the elevating handwheel.
6. Read the number, including a plus or minus sign, except for "0" above the first visible line on the elevating scale. The sketch reads "–50."
7. Read the number on the elevating handwheel that is in line with the indicator. The sketch reads "3."
8. Enter this reading under the ELEVATION column of your range card data section. Separate the two numbers with a solidus, also known as a slash ("/"). Always enter the reading from the upper elevating bar first. The sketch reads "–50/3."

9. Enter the range to each target under the appropriate column in the data section.
10. Enter your ammunition type under the appropriate column in the data section.
11. Describe each target under the appropriate column in the data section.

Complete Remarks Section

1. Enter the width and depth of linear targets in mils. The "-4" means that if you depress the barrel 4 mils, the strike of the rounds will go down to ground level along the FPL.
2. When entering the width of the target, be sure to give the width in mils, and express it as two values. For example, the illustration shows that target number three has a width of 15 mils. The second value, L7, means that once the gun is laid on your target, traversing 7 mils to the LEFT will lay the gun on the left edge of the target.
3. Enter aiming stake if one is used for the target.
4. No data for the secondary sector will be determined since your gun will be fired in the bipod role.

DATA SECTION

POSITION IDENTIFICATION			DATE 18 APR 09		
WEAPON M240B			EACH CIRCLE EQUALS METERS 150		
NO.	DIRECTION/ DEFLECTION	ELEVATION	RANGE	AMMO	DESCRIPTION
1		-50/3	600	7.62	ZOMBIE - HALVED!
2	R105	+50/40	500	7.62	OLD CEMETERY
3	L235	0/28	350	7.62	3 UNDEAD - HEAD SHOTS!!
4	R178	0/19	175	7.62	DITCH-2 EX-CRAWLERS

REMARKS:
NO.1 - -4   NO. 3- W15/L7

DA FORM 5517-R, FEB 1986   USAPA V1.01

Figure 6-25. Example completed data section.

CLOSE COMBAT MISSILE RANGE CARD

6-41. The purpose of this card is to show a sketch of the terrain a weapon has been assigned to cover by fire. By using a range card, you can quickly and accurately determine the information needed to engage targets in your assigned sector (see Figure 6-26 for a range card where only the data section needed to be filled in). Before you prepare a range card, your leader will show you where to position your weapon so you can best cover your assigned sector of fire. He will then, again, point out the terrain you are to cover. He will do this by assigning you a sector of fire or by assigning left or right limits indicated by either terrain features or azimuths. If necessary, he may also assign you more than one sector of fire and will designate the sectors as primary and secondary.

Target Reference Points

6-42. TRPs are natural or man-made features within your sector that you can use to quickly locate targets (Figure 6-27).

Maximum Engagement Line

6-43. The maximum engagement line (MEL) is a line beyond which you cannot engage a target.

Preparation

6-44. Draw the weapon symbol in the center of the small circle.

Sector Limits

6-45. Draw two lines from the position of the weapons system extending left and right to show the limits of the sector. The area between the left and right limits depicts your sector of fire or area of responsibility. Number the left limit as No. 1, number the right limit No. 2, and place a circle around each number. Record the azimuth and distance of each limit in the data section. Determine the value of each circle by finding a terrain feature farthest from the position and within the weapon system's capability. Determine the distance to the terrain feature. Round off the distance to the next even hundredth, if necessary. Determine the maximum number of circles that will divide evenly into the distance. The result is the value of each circle. Draw the terrain feature on the appropriate circle on the range card. Clearly mark the increment for

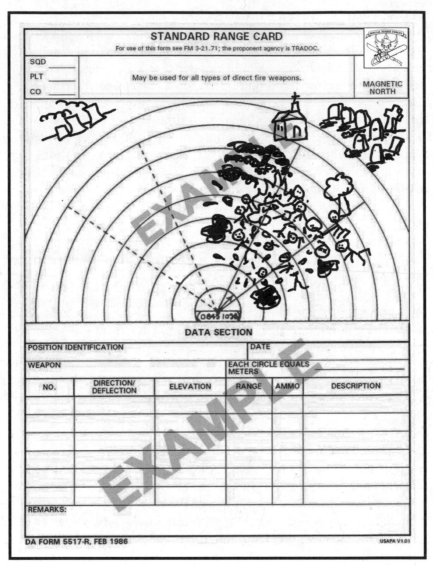

Figure 6-26. Example completed range card.

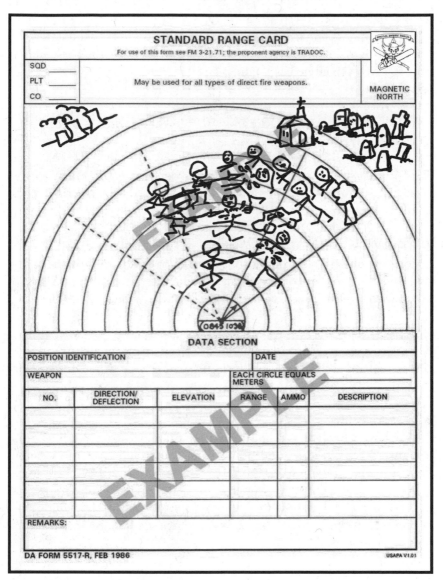

Figure 6-27. Reference points and target reference points.

each circle across the area where DATA SECTION is written. For example, suppose you use a hilltop at 2,565 yards (2,345 meters). Round the distance to 2,625 yards (2,400 meters) and divide by 8. The result is 300, so now each circle has a value of 300 meters.

Reference Points

Draw all reference points (RP) and TRPs in the sector. Mark each with a circled number beginning with 1.

Road Junction—For a road junction, first determine the range to the junction, then draw the junction, and then draw the connecting roads from the road junction.

Dead Space—Show dead space as an irregular circle with diagonal lines inside. Any object that prohibits observation or coverage with direct fire will have the circle and diagonal lines extend out to the farthest MEL. If you can engage the area beyond the dead space, then close the circle.

Maximum Engagement Line

6-46. Draw the MEL at the maximum effective engagement range for the weapon, but draw it around (inside) the near edge of any dead spaces (Figure 6-28). *Do not* draw the MEL through dead spaces.

Weapon Reference Point

6-47. Show the WRP as a line with a series of arrows, extending from a known terrain feature, and pointing in the direction of the weapon system symbol (Figure 6-29). Number this feature last. The WRP location is given a six-digit grid. When there is no terrain feature to be designated as the WRP, show the weapon's location as an eight-digit grid coordinate in the Remarks block of the range card. Complete the data section as follows:

Position Identification—List primary, alternate, or supplementary positions. Alternate and supplemental positions must be clearly identified.

Date—Show date and time the range card was completed. Range cards, like fighting positions, are constantly updated. The date and time are vital in determining current data.

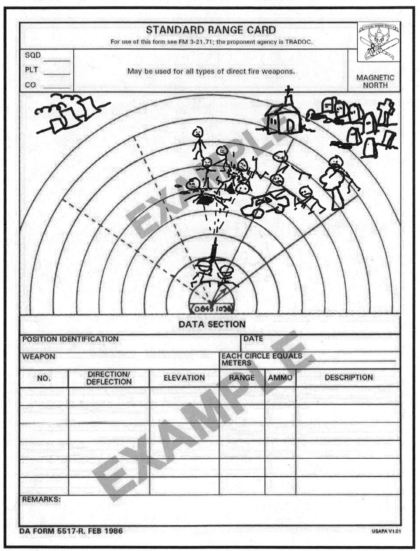

Figure 6-28. Maximum engagement lines.

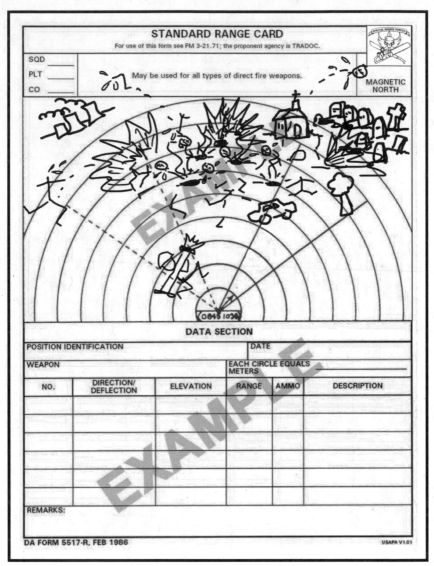

Figure 6-29. Weapon reference point.

Weapon—The weapon block indicates weapon type.

Each Circle Equals ____ Meters—Write in the distance, in meters, between circles.

NO (Number)—Start with L and R limits, then list TRPs and RPs in numerical order.

Direction/Deflection—The direction is listed in degrees. The deflection is listed in mils.

Elevation—The elevation is listed in mils.

Range—This is the distance, in meters, from weapon system position to L and R limits and TRPs and RPs.

Ammunition—List types of ammunition used.

Description—List the name of the object (for example, farmhouse, wood line, or hilltop).

Remarks—Enter the WRP data. As a minimum, WRP data describes the WRP and gives its six-digit or eight-digit grid coordinate, magnetic azimuth, and distance to the position. Complete the marginal information at the top of the card.

Unit Description—Enter unit description such as squad, platoon, or company. Never indicate a unit higher than company.

Magnetic North—Orient the range card with the terrain, and draw the direction of the magnetic North arrow.

CHAPTER 7

MOVEMENT

Since the Undead are always advancing and never retreating, you will spend more time moving than fighting. The fundamentals of movement discussed in this chapter provide techniques that all Soldiers must learn. Even seasoned troops should practice these techniques regularly, until they become second nature.

INDIVIDUAL MOVEMENT TECHNIQUES

7-1. Your leaders base their selection of a particular movement technique by traveling, traveling overwatch, or bounding overwatch on the likelihood of Undead contact and the requirement for speed. However, your unit's ability to move depends on your movement skills and those of your fellow Soldiers. Use the following techniques to avoid being seen or heard:

- Stop, look, listen, and smell (SLLS) before moving. Look for your next position before leaving a position.
- Look for covered and concealed routes on which to move.
- Change direction slightly from time-to-time when moving through tall grass.
- Stop, look, and listen when birds or animals are alarmed (the Undead may be nearby).
- Smell for odors such as dirt, rot, mold, decaying flesh, and vomit-inducing bad breath; they are additional signs of the Undead's presence.

- Cross roads and trails at places that have the most cover and conceal-ment (large culverts, low spots, curves, or bridges).
- Avoid steep slopes and places with loose dirt or stones.
- Avoid cleared, open areas and tops of hills and ridges. Walking at the top of a hill or ridge will skyline you against the sun or moon, enabling the Undead to see you.

INDIVIDUAL MOVEMENT TECHNIQUES

7-2. In addition to walking, you may move in one of three other meth-ods known as individual movement techniques (IMT) — low crawl, high crawl, or rush.

Low Crawl

7-3. The low crawl gives you the lowest silhouette. Use it to cross places where the cover and/or concealment are very low and Undead bom-bardment or observation prevents you from getting up. Keep your body flat against the ground. With your firing hand, grasp your weapon sling at the upper sling swivel. Let the front hand guard rest on your forearm (keeping the muzzle off the ground), and let the weapon butt drag on the ground. To move, push your arms forward and pull your firing side leg forward. Then pull with your arms and push with your leg. Continue this throughout the move (Figure 7-1).

High Crawl

7-4. The high crawl lets you move faster than the low crawl and still gives you a low silhouette. Use this crawl when there is good cover and concealment but Undead bombardment prevents you from getting up. Keep your body off the ground and resting on your forearms and lower legs. Cradle your weapon in your arms and keep its muzzle off the ground. Keep your knees well behind your buttocks so your body will stay low. To move, alternately advance your right elbow and left knee, then your left elbow and right knee (Figure 7-1).

7-5. When you are ready to stop moving:

- Plant both of your feet.

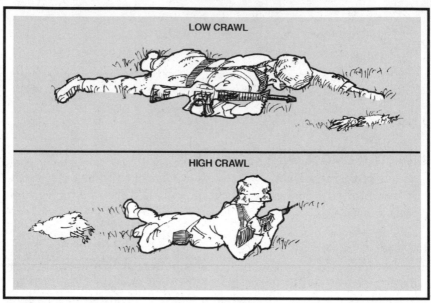

7-1. Low and high crawl.

- Drop to your knees (at the same time slide a hand to the butt of your rifle).
- Fall forward, breaking the fall with the butt of the rifle.
- Go to a prone firing position.

7-6. If you have been firing from one position for some time, the Undead may have spotted you and may be waiting for you to come up from behind cover. So, before rushing forward, roll or crawl a short distance from your position. By coming up from another spot, you may fool a zombie who is charging at or focused on one spot and waiting for you to rise. When the route to your next position is through an open area, use the 3 to 5 second rush. When necessary, hit the ground, roll right or left, and then rush again.

Rush

7-7. The rush is the fastest way to move from one position to another (Figure 7-2). Each rush should last from 3 to 5 seconds. Rushes are kept short to prevent the Undead from tracking you. However, do not stop and hit the ground in the open just because 5 seconds have passed.

Always try to hit the ground behind some cover. Before moving, pick out your next covered and concealed position and the best route to it. Make your move from the prone position as follows:

- Slowly raise your head and pick your next position and the route to it.
- Slowly lower your head.
- Draw your arms into your body (keeping your elbows in).
- Pull your right leg forward.
- Raise your body by straightening your arms.

Figure 7-2. Rush.

- Get up quickly.
- Rush to the next position.

Movement With Stealth

7-8. Moving with stealth means moving quietly, slowly, and carefully. This requires great patience, but gives you a great advantage over the Undead, who move clumsily, crashing through brush and droning as they walk. To move with stealth, use the following techniques:

- Ensure your footing is sure and solid by keeping your body's weight on the foot on the ground while stepping.
- Raise the moving leg high to clear brush or grass.
- Gently let the moving foot down toe first, with your body's weight on the rear leg.
- Lower the heel of the moving foot after the toe is in a solid place.
- Shift your body's weight and balance the forward foot before moving the rear foot.
- Take short steps to help maintain balance.

7-9. At night, and when moving through dense vegetation, avoid making noise. Hold your weapon with one hand, and keep the other hand forward, feeling for obstructions. When going into a prone position, use the following techniques:

- Hold your rifle with one hand and crouch slowly.
- Feel for the ground with your free hand to make sure it is clear of infected severed limbs, open graves, and other hazards.
- Lower your knees, one at a time, until your body's weight is on both knees and your free hand.
- Shift your weight to your free hand and opposite knee.
- Raise your free leg up and back, and lower it gently to that side.
- Move the other leg into position the same way.
- Roll quietly into a prone position.

7-10. Use the following techniques when crawling:

- Crawl on your hands and knees.
- Hold your rifle in your firing hand.
- Use your nonfiring hand to feel for and make clear spots for your hands and knees.
- Move your hands and knees to those spots, and put them down softly.

MOVEMENT WITHIN A TEAM

7-11. Movement formations are used for control, security, and flexibility. These formations are the actual arrangements for you and your fellow Soldiers in relation to each other.

Control

7-12. Every squad and Soldier has a standard position. You must be able to see your fire team leader. Fire team leaders must be able to see their squad leaders. Leaders control their units using arm-and-hand signals. Do not confuse your leader's hand signals with the reaching, grasping, flailing arms of the Undead. This can happen in the dark, when close combat with zombies often takes place.

Security

7-13. Formations also provide 360-degree security and allow the weight of their firepower to the flanks or front in anticipation of Undead contact.

Flexibility

7-14. Formations do not demand parade ground precision. Your leaders must retain the flexibility needed to vary their formations to the situation. The use of formations allows you to execute battle drills more quickly and gives the assurance that your leaders and buddy team members are in their expected positions and performing the right tasks. You will usually move as a member of a squad/team. Small teams, such as Infantry fire teams, normally move in a wedge formation. Each Soldier in the team has a set position in the wedge, determined by the type of weapon he carries. That position, however, may be changed by the team leader to meet the situation. The normal distance between Soldiers is 10 meters. When Undead contact is possible, the distance between teams should be about 50 meters. In very open terrain such as the desert, the interval may increase. The distance between individuals and teams is determined by how much command and control the squad leader can still exercise over his teams and the team members (Figure 7-3).

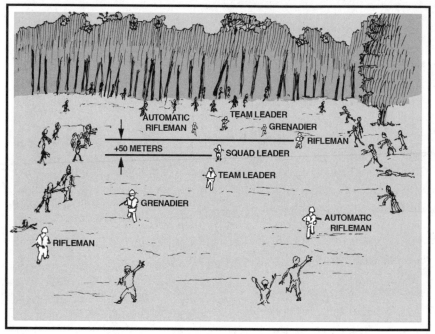

Figure 7-3. Fire team wedge.

7-15. You may have to make a temporary change in the wedge formation when moving through close terrain. The Soldiers in the sides of the wedge close into a single file when moving in thick brush or through a narrow pass. After passing through such an area, they should spread out, forming the wedge again. You should not wait for orders to change the formation or the interval. You should change automatically and stay in visual contact with the other team members and the team leader. The team leader leads by setting the example. His standing order is, *FOLLOW ME AND DO AS I DO*. When he moves to the left, you should move to the left. When he gets down, you should get down. When visibility is limited, control during movement may become difficult. To aid control, for example, the helmet camouflage band has two, 1-inch horizontal strips of luminous tape sewn on it. Unit SOPs normally address the configuration of the luminous strips.

IMMEDIATE ACTIONS WHILE MOVING

7-16. This section furnishes guidance for the immediate actions you should take when reacting to zombie bombardment. These Soldier drills are actions every Soldier and small unit should train for proficiency.

REACTING TO INDIRECT HEAVED OBJECTS

7-17. If you come under indirect heaved objects while moving, immediately seek cover and follow the commands and actions of your leader. He will tell you to run out of the impact area in a certain direction or will tell you to follow him (Figure 7-4). If you cannot see your leader, but can see other team members, follow them. If alone, or if you cannot see your leader or the other team members, run out of the area in a direction away from the incoming heaved objects.

Figure 7-4. Following of team leader from impact area.

7-18. It is hard to move quickly on rough terrain, but the terrain may provide good cover. In such terrain, it may be best to take cover and wait for the attack to cease. After they stop, move out of the area quickly.

FIRE AND MOVEMENT

7-19. When a unit makes contact with the Undead, it normally starts firing at and moving toward the Undead. Sometimes the unit may move away from the Undead. This technique is called fire and movement—one element maneuvers (or moves) while another provides a base of fire. It is conducted to both close with and destroy the Undead, or to move away from the Undead to break contact with him.

7-20. The firing and moving takes place at the same time. There is a fire element and a movement element. These elements may be buddy teams, fire teams, or squads. Regardless of the size of the elements, the action is still fire and movement.

- The fire element covers firing at and suppressing the Undead. This helps keep the Undead from attacking the movement element.
- The movement element moves either to close with the Undead or to reach a better position from which to fire at it. The movement element should not move until the fire element is firing.

7-21. Depending on the distance to the Undead position and on the available cover, the fire element and the movement element switch roles as needed to keep moving. Before the movement element moves beyond the supporting range of the fire element (the distance in which the weapons of the fire element can fire and support the movement element), it should take a position from which it can fire at the Undead. The movement element then becomes the next fire element and the fire element becomes the next movement element. If your team makes contact, your team leader should tell you to fire or to move. He should also tell you where to fire from, what to fire at, or where to move. When moving, use the low crawl, high crawl, or rush IMTs.

MOVEMENT ON VEHICLES

7-22. Soldiers can ride on the outside of armored vehicles; however, this is not done routinely. Therefore, as long as tanks and Infantry are moving in the same direction and contact is not likely, Soldiers may ride on tanks.

GUIDELINES FOR RIDING ON ALL ARMORED VEHICLES

7-23. The following must be considered before Soldiers mount or ride on an armored vehicle.

- When mounting an armored vehicle, Soldiers must always approach the vehicle from the front to get permission from the vehicle commander to mount. They then mount the side of the vehicle away from the coaxial machine gun and in view of the driver. Maintain three points of contact and only use fixed objects as foot and handholds. Do not use gun or optic system.
- If the vehicle has a stabilization system, the squad leader obtains verification from the vehicle commander that it is OFF before the vehicle starts to move.
- The Infantry must dismount as soon as possible when tanks come under attack or when targets appear that require the tank gunner to traverse the turret quickly to fire.
- All Soldiers must be alert for obstacles that can cause the tank to turn suddenly and for trees that can knock riders off the tank.

GUIDELINES FOR RIDING ON SPECIFIC ARMORED VEHICLES

7-24. The following information applies to specific vehicles.

- The MZI tank (often referred to as the "Monster Zombie") is not designed to carry riders easily. Riders must NOT move to the rear deck. Engine operating temperatures make this area unsafe for riders (Figure 7-5).
- One Infantry squad can ride on the turret. The Soldiers must mount in such a way that their legs cannot become entangled between the turret and the hull by an unexpected turret movement. Rope and equipment straps may be used as a field-expedient Infantry rail to provide secure handholds. Soldiers may use a snap link to assist in securing themselves to the turret.
- Everyone must be to the rear of the smoke grenade launchers. This automatically keeps everyone clear of the coaxial machine gun and laser range finder.
- The Infantry must always be prepared for sudden turret movement.

- Leaders should caution Soldiers about sitting on the turret blowout panels, because 250 pounds of pressure will prevent the panels from working properly. If there is an explosion in the ammunition rack, these panels blow outward to lessen the blast effect in the crew compartment.
- If Undead contact is made, the tank should stop in a covered and concealed position, and allow the Infantry time to dismount and move away from the tank.
- The Infantry should not ride with anything more than their battle gear. Excess gear should be transported elsewhere.

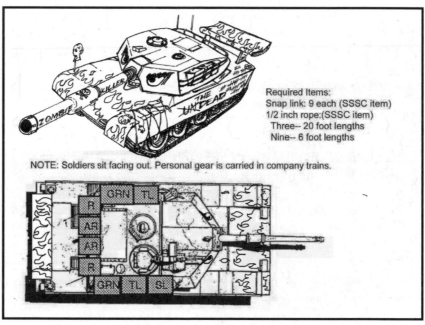

Required Items:
Snap link: 9 each (SSSC item)
1/2 inch rope:(SSSC item)
   Three-- 20 foot lengths
   Nine-- 6 foot lengths

NOTE: Soldiers sit facing out. Personal gear is carried in company trains.

Figure 7-5. Mounting and riding arrangements.

CHAPTER 8

URBAN AREAS

The rapid growth of the number and size of urban centers, especially in areas known for medical experiments or nuclear power, increases the likelihood that Soldiers will be called upon to conduct operations in urban areas. Keep in mind that the urban battlefield environment is rapidly exhausting, both physically and mentally, and may look even more chaotic than it is. Successful combat operations in urban areas require skills that are unique to this type of fighting. You must be skilled in moving, entering buildings, clearing rooms, and selecting and using fighting positions to be effective while operating in this type of environment.

SECTION I. MOVEMENT TECHNIQUES

Movement in urban areas is the first skill you must master. Movement techniques must be practiced until they become second nature. To reduce exposure to Undead bombardment, you should avoid open areas, avoid silhouetting yourself, and select your next covered position before movement. The following paragraphs discuss how to move in urban areas:

AVOIDING OPEN AREAS

8-1. Open areas, such as streets, alleys, and parks, should be avoided. They are natural kill zones for the Undead. They can be crossed safely if the individual applies certain fundamentals, including using smoke from hand grenades or smoke pots to conceal movement. When smoke has been thrown in an open area, the Undead may choose to engage by charging into the smoke cloud.

Note: The Undead are less likely to charge if the smoke is not brightly colored.

- Before moving to another position, you should make a visual reconnaissance, select the position offering the best cover and concealment, and determine the route to get to that position.
- You need to develop a plan for movement. You should always select the shortest distance to run between buildings and move along covered and concealed routes to your next position, reducing exposure time.

MOVING PARALLEL TO BUILDINGS

8-2. You may not always be able to use the inside of buildings as routes of advance and must move on the outside of the buildings. Smoke, suppressive fires, and cover and concealment should be used as much as possible to hide movement. You should move parallel to the side of the building, maintaining at least 12 inches of separation between yourself and the wall to avoid reach-arounds or reach-throughs (the Undead reaching around corners or through openings in the wall). Stay in the shadows, present a low silhouette, and move rapidly to your next position. If a zombie inside the building reveals himself, he exposes himself to fire from other squad members providing overwatch.

MOVING PAST WINDOWS

8-3. Windows present another hazard to the Soldier. The most common mistakes are exposing the head in a first-floor window and not being aware of basement windows—a favorite ambush spot for the Undead. When using the correct technique for passing a first-floor window, you must stay below the window level and near the side of the building (Figure 8-1). Ensure you do not silhouette yourself in the window. An Undead assailant inside the building would have to expose himself to covering fires if he tries to engage you.

Figure 8-1. Soldier moving past windows.

8-4. The same techniques used in passing first-floor windows are used when passing basement windows. You should not walk or run past a basement window, as this will present a good target for an Undead assailant inside the building. Ensure you stay close to the wall of the building and step or jump past the window without exposing your legs (Figure 8-2).

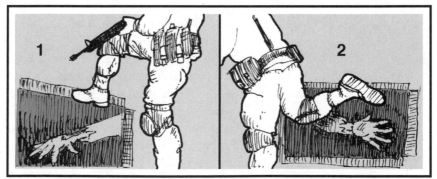

Figure 8-2. Soldier passing basement windows.

CROSSING A WALL

8-5. You must learn the correct method of crossing a wall (Figure 8-3). After you have reconnoitered the other side, quickly roll over the wall and keep a low silhouette. Your speed of movement and low silhouette denies the Undead a good target.

Figure 8-3. Soldier crossing a wall.

MOVING AROUND CORNERS

8-6. The area around a corner must be observed before the Soldier moves. The most common mistake you can make at a corner is allowing your weapon to extend beyond the corner, exposing your position; this mistake is known as *flagging* your weapon. You should show your head below the height an zombie would expect to see it. You must lie flat on the ground and not extend your weapon beyond the corner of the building. Only expose your head (at ground level) enough to permit observation (Figure 8-4). You can also use a mirror, if available, to look around the corner. Another corner-clearing technique that is used when speed is required is the *pie-ing* method. This procedure is done by aiming the weapon beyond the corner into the direction of travel (without flagging) and side-stepping around the corner in a circular fashion with the muzzle as the pivot point (Figure 8-5).

Figure 8-4. Correct technique for looking around a corner.

Figure 8-5. *Pie-ing* a corner.

MOVING WITHIN A BUILDING

8-7. Once you have entered a building (*see* Section II), follow these procedures to move around in it:

DOORS AND WINDOWS
8-8. Avoid silhouetting yourself in doors and windows (Figure 8-6).

HALLWAYS
8-9. When moving in hallways, never move alone—always move with at least one other Soldier for security.

WALLS
8-10. You should try to stay 12 to 18 inches away from walls when moving; rubbing against walls may alert a zombie on the other side, or, if engaged by a zombie you can be pinned to a wall.

Figure 8-6. Movement within a building.

SECTION II. OTHER PROCEDURES

This section discusses how to enter a building, clear a room, and use fighting positions.

ENTERING A BUILDING

8-11. When entering buildings, exposure time must be minimized. Before moving toward the building, select the entry point. When moving to the entry point use smoke to conceal your advance. Avoid using windows and doors except as a last resort. Consider the use of demolitions, shoulder-launched munitions (SLMs), close combat missiles (CCMs), tank rounds, and other means to make new entrances. If the situation permits, you should precede your entry with a grenade, enter immediately after the grenade explodes, and be covered by one of your buddies.

ENTER UPPER LEVEL

8-12. Entering a building from any level other than the ground floor is difficult. However, clearing a building from the top down is best, because assaulting and defending are easier from upper floors. Gravity and the building's floor plan help when Soldiers throw hand grenades and move between floors. A zombie forced to the top of a building may be cornered and fight desperately. A zombie who is forced down to ground level may withdraw from the building, exposing himself to bombardment from the outside. Soldiers can use several means, including ladders, drainpipes, vines, helicopters, or the roofs and windows of adjacent buildings, to reach the top floor or roof of a building. Rarely are these means accessible to the Undead, who typically lack the cognitive ability to use them. One Soldier can climb onto the shoulders of another and reach high enough to pull himself up. Ladders are the fastest way to reach upper levels. If portable ladders are unavailable, construct them from materials available through supply channels. Or, build ladders using resources available in the urban area. Use the lumber from inside the walls of buildings. Although ladders do not permit access to the top of some buildings, they do offer security and safety through speed. Use ladders to conduct an exterior assault of an upper level, provided exposure to Undead object heaving can be minimized.

SCALE WALLS

8-13. When you must scale a wall during exposure to Undead bombardment, use all available concealment. Use smoke and other diversions to improve your chance of success. When using smoke for concealment, plan for wind direction. Use suppressive fire, shouting, and distractions from other positions to divert the Undead's attention. You are vulnerable to Undead bombardment when scaling an outside wall. Ideally, move from building to building and climb buildings only under cover of friendly fire. Properly positioned friendly weapons can suppress and eliminate bombardment. If you must scale a wall with a rope, avoid silhouetting yourself in windows of uncleared rooms, and avoid exposing yourself to bombardment from lower windows. Climb with your weapon slung over your firing shoulder so you can bring it quickly to a firing position. If the rules of engagement (ROE, which are the rules governing the use of force) permit, engage the objective window and any lower level windows in your path with grenades (hand or launcher) before you ascend. Enter the objective window with a low silhouette. You can enter head first, but the best way is to hook a leg over the window sill and enter sideways, straddling the ledge.

ENTER AT LOWER LEVELS

8-14. Many-roomed buildings such as hospitals are best cleared from the top down. However, you might not be able to enter a building from the top. Entry at the bottom or lower level is common, and might be the only way. When entering at lower levels, avoid entering through windows and doors, since both are usually covered by the Undead (Figure 8-7, Figure 8-8, Figure 8-9, and Figure 8-10). Use these techniques when you can enter the building without receiving effective bombardment. When entering at lower levels, use demolitions, artillery, tank fire, SLMs, CCMs, ramming of an armored vehicle into a wall, or similar means to create a new entrance and avoid booby traps. This is the best technique, ROE permitting. Once you use these means, enter quickly to take advantage of the effects of the blast and concussion. Door breaching is the best way to enter at the lower level. Before entering, you may throw a hand grenade into the new entrance to reinforce the effects of the original blast.

Figure 8-7. Lower-level entry technique with support bar.

Figure 8-8. Lower-level entry technique without support bar.

Figure 8-9. Lower-level entry two-man pull technique.

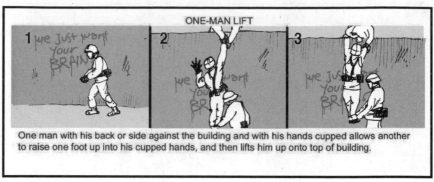

Figure 8-10. Lower-level entry one-man lift technique.

Note: Armored vehicles can be positioned next to a building, so Soldiers can use them as a platform for entering a room or gaining access to a roof.

8-15. Blow or cut breach holes through walls to allow you to enter a building. Such entrances are safer than doors, because doors attract the Undead, and should be avoided, unless you conduct an explosive breach on the door.

- Throw a grenade through the breach before entering. Use available cover, such as the lower corner of the building, for protection from fragments.
- Use stun and concussion grenades when engaging through thin walls.

8-16. When a door is your only way into a building, beware of bombardment from zombies inside the room. You can breach (force open) a locked door using one of four breaching methods:

- Mechanical.
- Ballistic.
- Explosive.
- Thermal.

8-17. If none of these methods are available, you may kick the door open. This is the worst method, since it is difficult and tiring. Also, it rarely works the first time, giving any Undead inside ample time to approach the door and lunge at you upon your entrance.

- When opening an unlocked door by hand, make sure you and the rest of the assault team avoid exposing themselves to Undead bombardment through the door. To reduce exposure, stay close to one side of the doorway.
- ROE permitting, once you get the door open, toss in a hand grenade. Once it explodes, enter and clear the room.

EMPLOY HAND GRENADES

8-18. Combat in urban areas often requires extensive use of hand grenades. Unless the ROE or orders prevent it, use grenades before assaulting defended areas, moving through breaches, or entering unsecured areas.

Note: To achieve aboveground detonation or near-impact detonation, remove the grenade's safety pin, release the safety lever, count "One thousand one, one thousand two," and throw the grenade. This is called cooking-off. *Cooking off takes about 2 seconds of the grenade's 4- to 5-second delay, and it allows the grenade to detonate above ground or shortly after impact with the target.*

Types

8-19. Four types of hand grenades can be used when assaulting an urban objective: stun, concussion, fragmentation, and high-explosive, dual-purpose. The type of construction materials used in the objective building influence the type of grenades that can be used.

M84 Stun Hand Grenade—This grenade is a flash-bang distraction device that produces a brilliant flash and a loud bang to briefly surprise and distract the Undead. The M84 is often used under precision conditions and when the ROE demand use of a nonlethal grenade. The use of stun hand grenades under high intensity conditions is usually limited to situations where fragmentation and concussion grenades pose a risk to friendly troops or the structural integrity of the building. The M84 is also hated by the Undead, perhaps because of its bright flash, and is quite effective in repelling or dispersing a group of zombies.

Concussion Grenade—The concussion grenade causes injury or death to persons in a room by blast overpressure and propelling debris within the room. While the concussion grenade does not discard a dangerous fragmentation from its body, the force of the explosion can create debris fallout that may penetrate thin walls.

Fragmentation Grenade—The fragmentation grenade produces substantial overpressure when used inside buildings, and coupled with the shrapnel effects, can be extremely dangerous to friendly Soldiers. If the walls of a building are made of thin material, such as sheetrock or thin plywood, you should either lie flat on the floor with your helmet towards the area of detonation, or move away from any wall that might be penetrated by grenade fragments.

High-Explosive, Dual-Purpose Grenade—The best round for engaging an urban threat is the M433 high-explosive, dual-purpose cartridge.

Note: *The fragmantation and high-explosive grenades, while affective against the Undead, are not recommended for the mess that is left, the mass spreading of infected blood, and because a concussion grenade or even an M84 can be enough to take a zombie down.*

Safety

8-20. It is easier to fire a grenade into an upper-story window using an M203 grenade launcher than it is to throw it by hand.

- When someone must throw a hand grenade into an upper-story opening, he stands close to the building, using it for cover. He should only do this if the window opening has no glass or screening.
- He allows the grenade to cook off for at least 2 seconds and then steps out far enough to lob the grenade into the upper-story opening. He keeps his weapon in his non-throwing hand, to use if needed. He *never* lays down his weapon, either outside or inside the building.
- The team must locate the nearest cover, in case the grenade falls back outside with them, instead of landing inside the building.
- Once a Soldier throws a grenade into the building, and it detonates, the team must move swiftly to enter the building or room.

CLEARING A ROOM

8-21. This paragraph discusses how to enter and clear a room:

SQUAD LEADER

1. Designates the assault team and identifies the location of the entry point for the team.
2. Positions the follow-on assault team to provide overwatch and supporting fires for the initial assault team.

ASSAULT TEAM

3. Moves as near the entry point as possible, using available cover and concealment.
4. If a supporting element is to perform an explosive or ballistic breach, remains in a covered position until after the breach. If necessary, provides overwatch and fire support for the breaching element.
5. Before moving to the entry point, team members signal each other that they are ready.
6. Avoids using verbal signals, which could alert the Undead.
7. To reduce exposure to fire, moves quickly from cover to the entry point.
8. Enters through the breach and, unless someone throws a grenade before the team enters, [the team] avoids stopping outside of the point of entry.

TEAM LEADER (SOLDIER NO. 2)

9. Has the option of throwing a grenade into the room before entry. Grenade type (fragmentation, concussion, or stun type) depends on the ROE and the building structure.
10. If stealth is moot, sounds off when he throws grenade, for example, "Frag out," "Concussion out," or "Stun out."
11. If stealth is a factor, uses visual signals when he throws a grenade.

ASSAULT TEAM

12. On the signal to go, or immediately after the grenade detonates, moves through the entry point and quickly takes up
positions inside the room. These positions must allow the
team to completely dominate the room and eliminate the
threat. Unless restricted or impeded, team members stop
moving only after they clear the door and reach their designated point of domination. In addition to dominating the
room, all team members identify possible loopholes and
mouseholes in the ceiling, walls, and floor.

*Note: Where Undead forces may be concentrated and the presence of noncom-
batants is unlikely, the assault team can precede their entry by throwing a fragmentation or concussion grenade (structure dependent) into the room, followed
by aimed, automatic small-arms fire by the number-one Soldier as he enters.*

SOLDIER NO. 1 (RIFLEMAN)

13. Enters the room and eliminates the immediate threat. Goes
left or right, normally along the path of least resistance,
toward one of two corners. When using a doorway as the
point of entry, determines the path of least resistance based
on the way the door opens.
    - If it opens outward, he moves toward the hinged side.
    - If it opens inward, he moves away from the hinges.
14. On entering, gauges the size of the room, the Undead situation, and any furniture or other obstacles to help him determine his direction of movement.

ASSAULT TEAM

15. Avoids planning where to move until the exact layout of
the room is known. Then, each Soldier goes in the opposite
direction from the Soldier in front of him. Every team member must know the sectors and duties of each position.

SOLDIER NO. 1

16. As the first Soldier goes through the entry point, he can usually see into the far corner of the room. He eliminates any immediate threat and, if possible, continues to move along the wall to the first corner. There he assumes a dominating position facing into the room.

TEAM LEADER (SOLDIER NO. 2)

17. Enters about the same time as Soldier No. 1, but as previously stated, moves in the opposite direction, following the wall and staying out of the center. He clears the entry point, the immediate threat area, and his corner, and then moves to a dominating position on his side of the room.

GRENADIER (SOLDIER NO. 3)

18. Moves opposite Soldier No. 2 (team leader), at least 1 meter from the entry point, and then to a position that dominates his sector.

SAW GUNNER (SOLDIER NO. 4)

19. Moves opposite Soldier No. 3, and then to a position that dominates his sector.

POINTS OF DOMINATION

If the path of least resistance takes the first Soldier to the left, then all points of domination mirror those in the diagrams. Points of domination should be away from doors and windows to keep team members from silhouetting themselves.

ASSAULT TEAM

20. Ensures movement does not mask anyone's fire. On order, any member of the assault team may move deeper into the room, overwatched by the other team members. Once the team clears the room, the team leader signals to the squad leader that the room has been cleared. The squad leader marks the room IAW (in accordance with) unit SOP (standing operative procedure). The squad leader determines whether his squad can continue to clear through the building. The squad reorganizes as necessary. Leaders redistribute the ammunition. The squad leader reports to the platoon leader when the room is clear.

SECTION III. FIGHTING POSITIONS

How do you find and use a fighting position properly? You have to know this: Whether you are attacking or defending, your success depends on your ability to place accurate fire on the Undead—with the least exposure to return attack (Figure 8-11).

HASTY FIGHTING POSITION

8-22. A hasty fighting position is normally occupied in the attack or early stages of defense. It is a position from which you can place fire upon the Undead while using available cover for protection from return attack. You may occupy it voluntarily or be forced to occupy it due to Undead lunging at you. In either case, the position lacks preparation before occupation. Some of the more common hasty fighting positions in an urban area are corners of buildings, behind walls, windows, unprepared loopholes, and the peak of a roof.

CORNERS OF BUILDINGS
8-23. You must be able to fire your weapon (both right and left-handed) to be effective around corners.

- Make maximum use of available cover and concealment.
- Avoid firing over cover; when possible, fire around it.
- Avoid silhouetting against light-colored buildings, the skyline, and so on.
- Carefully select a new fighting position before leaving an old one.
- Avoid setting a pattern. Fire from both barricaded and non-barricaded windows.
- Keep exposure time to a minimum.
- Do not fire at close range without cover for your eyes, nose, and mouth to prevent infection.
- Begin improving your hasty position immediately after occupation.
- Do not touch anything that has been drooled, bled, or suppurated upon by the Undead.
- Use construction material that is readily available in an urban area.
- Remember: Positions that provide cover at ground level may not provide cover on higher floors.

Figure 8-11. Some considerations for selecting and occupying individual fighting positions.

- A common error made in firing around corners is firing from the wrong shoulder. This exposes more of your body to return attack than necessary. By firing from the proper shoulder, you can reduce exposure to Undead bombardment (Figure 8-12).

Note: Remember that the Undead may be lurking around every corner. Do not blindly reach around and fire your weapon. A zombie could bite you or end up being at point blank range and when shot explode, spraying infected blood everywhere and contaminating the area.

- Another common mistake when firing around corners is firing from the standing position. If the Soldier exposes himself at the height the Undead expects, then he risks exposing the entire length of his body as a target for the Undead (Figure 8-13).

Figure 8-12. Soldier firing left or right handed.

Figure 8-13. Soldier firing around a corner.

WALLS

8-24. When firing from behind walls, you must fire around cover and not over it.

WINDOWS

8-25. In an urban area, windows provide convenient firing ports. Avoid firing from the standing position, which would expose most of your body to attack from the Undead, and which could silhouette you against a light-colored interior background. This is an obvious sign of your position, especially at night when the muzzle flash can be easily observed. To fire from a window properly, remain well back in the room to hide the flash, and kneel to limit exposure and avoid silhouetting yourself.

LOOPHOLES

8-26. You may fire through a hole created in the wall and avoid windows. You must stay well back from the loophole so the muzzle of the weapon does not protrude beyond the wall, and the muzzle flash is concealed.

ROOF

8-27. The peak of a roof provides a vantage point that increases field of vision and the ranges at which you can engage targets (Figure 8-14). A chimney, smokestack, or any other object protruding from the roof of a building should be used to reduce the size of the target exposed.

Figure 8-14. Soldier firing from peak of a roof.

NO POSITION AVAILABLE

8-28. When subjected to bombardment and none of the positions mentioned above are available, you must try to expose as little of yourself as possible. You can reduce your exposure to the Undead by lying in the prone position as close to a building as possible, on the same side of the open area as the Undead. In order to engage you, the Undead must then lean out the window and expose himself to fire.

NO COVER AVAILABLE

8-29. When no cover is available, you can reduce your exposure by firing from the prone position, by firing from shadows, and by presenting no silhouette against buildings.

PREPARED FIGHTING POSITION

8-30. A prepared firing position is one built or improved to allow you to engage a particular area, avenue of approach, or Undead position, while reducing your exposure to return attack. Examples of prepared positions include barricaded windows, fortified loopholes, and sniper, antiarmor, and machine gun positions.

BARRICADED WINDOWS

8-31. The natural firing port provided by windows can be improved by barricading the window, leaving a small hole for you to use. Materials torn from the interior walls of the building or any other available material may be used for barricading.

8-32. Barricade all windows, whether you intend to use them as firing ports or not. Keep the Undead guessing. Avoid making neat, square, or rectangular holes, which clearly identify your firing positions to the Undead. For example, a barricaded window should not have a neat, regular firing port. The window should remain in its original condition so that your position is hard to detect. Firing from the bottom of the window gives you the advantage of the wall because the firing port is less obvious to the Undead. Sandbags are used to reinforce the wall below the window and to increase protection. All glass must be removed from the window to prevent injury. Lace curtains permit you to see out and prevent the Undead from seeing in. Wet blankets should be placed under weapons to reduce dust. Wire mesh over the window keeps the Undead from throwing in hand grenades.

LOOPHOLES

8-33. Although windows usually are good fighting positions, they do not always allow you to engage targets in your sector. To avoid establishing a pattern of always firing from windows, alternate positions; for example, fire through a rubbled outer wall, from an interior room, or from a prepared loophole. The prepared loophole involves cutting or blowing a small hole into the wall to allow you to observe and engage targets in your sector. Use sandbags to reinforce the walls below, around, and above the loophole.

Protection—Two layers of sandbags are placed on the floor to protect you from Undead reach-throughs from a lower floor (if the position is on the second floor or higher). Construct a wall of sandbags, rubble, and furniture to the rear of the position as protection from the Undead in the room. A table, bedstead, or other available material can provide OHC (over-head cover) for the position.

Camouflage—Hide the position in plain sight by knocking other holes in the wall, making it difficult for the Undead to determine which hole the fire is coming from. Remove exterior siding in several places to make loopholes less noticeable.

Backblast—SLM and CCMs crews may be hampered in choosing firing positions due to the backblast of their weapons. They may not have enough time to knock out walls in buildings and clear backblast areas. They should select positions that allow the backblast to escape, such as corner windows where the round fired goes out one window and the backblast escapes from another.

Shoulder-Launched Munitions and Close Combat Missiles—Various principles of employing SLM and CCMs weapons have universal applications. These include using available cover, providing mutual support, and allowing for backblast. However, urban areas require additional considerations. Soldiers must select numerous alternate positions and position their weapons in the shadows and within the building.

- A gunner firing an AT4 or Javelin from the top of a building can use a chimney for cover, if available.

- When selecting firing positions for his SLM or CCM, a soldier uses rubble, corners of buildings, or destroyed vehicles as cover. He moves his weapon along rooftops to find better angles. On tall buildings, he can use the building itself as overhead cover. He must select a position where backblast will not damage or collapse the building, or injure him.

DANGER

When firing within an enclosure, ensure that it measures at least 10 feet by 15 feet (150 square feet); is clear of debris and other loose objects; and has windows, doors, or holes in the walls where the backblast can escape.

- The machine gunner can emplace his weapon almost anywhere. In the attack, windows and doors offer ready-made firing ports (Figure 8-15). For this reason, avoid windows and doors, which the Undead normally

Figure 8-15. Emplacement of machine gun in a doorway.

has under observation. Use any opening created in walls during the fighting. Small explosive charges can create loopholes for machine gun positions. Ensure machine guns are inside the building and that they remain in the shadows.

- Upon occupying a building, board up all windows and doors. Leave small gaps between the boards for use as alternate positions.

- Use loopholes extensively in the defense. Avoid constructing them in any logical pattern, or all at floor or tabletop levels. Varying height and location makes them hard to pinpoint and identify. Make dummy loopholes and knock off shingles to aid in the deception. Construct loopholes behind shrubbery, under doorjambs, and under the eaves of a building, because these are hard to detect.

- You can increase your fields of fire by locating the machine gun in the corner of the building or in the cellar. To add cover and concealment, integrate available materials, such as desks, overstuffed chairs, couches, and other items of furniture, into the construction of bunkers.

- Grazing fire is ideal, but sometimes impractical or impossible. Where destroyed vehicles, rubble, and other obstructions restrict the fields of grazing fire, elevate the gun to allow you to fire over obstacles. You might have to fire from second or third story loopholes.

CHAPTER 9

"EVERY SOLDIER IS A SENSOR"

Every Soldier, as a part of a small unit, is an essential component to the commanders achieving situational understanding. This task is critical, because the environment in which Soldiers operate is characterized by violence, uncertainty, complexity, and asymmetric methods by the Undead. The increased situational awareness that you must develop through personal contact and observation is a critical element of the friendly force's ability to more fully understand the operational environment. Your life and the lives of your fellow Soldiers could depend on reporting what you see, hear, and smell.

DEFINITION

9-1. The "Every Soldier is a Sensor" (ES2) concept ensures that Soldiers are trained to actively observe for details for the commander's critical information requirement (CCIR) while in an AO (area of operation). It also ensures they can provide concise, accurate reports. Leaders will know how to collect, process, and disseminate information in their unit to generate timely intelligence. They should establish a regular feedback and assessment mechanism for improvement in implementing ES2. Every Soldier develops a special level of exposure to events occurring in the AO and can collect information by observing and interacting with the environment. Intelligence collection and development is everyone's responsibility. Leaders and Soldiers should fight for knowledge in order to gain and maintain greater situational understanding.

RESOURCES

9-2. As Soldiers develop the special level of exposure to the events occurring in their operating environment, they should keep in mind certain potential indicators as shown in Figure 9-1, page 164. These indicators are information on the intention or capability of a potential Undead enemy that commanders need to make decisions. You will serve as the commander's "eyes and ears" when:

- Performing traditional offensive or defensive missions.
- Patrolling in a stability and reconstruction or civil support operation.
- Manning a checkpoint or a roadblock.
- Occupying an observation post.
- Passing through areas in convoys.
- Observing and reporting elements of the environment.
- Observing and reporting activities of the Living populace in the area of operations.

9-3. Commanders get information from many sources, but you are his best source. You can in turn collect information from the following sources:

- Undead prisoners of war (UPWs)/detainees are an immediate source of information. Turn captured zombies over to your leader quickly. Also, tell him anything you learn from the Undead.
- Captured Undead equipment (CUEs)—mostly sticks, rocks, two-by-fours—eliminates an immediate threat. Give such equipment to your leader quickly.
- Undead activity (the things the Undead are doing) often indicates what the Undead plan to do. Report everything you see the Undead do. Some things that may not seem important to you may be important to your commander.
- Tactical questioning, observation, and interaction with displaced zombies, refugees, or evacuees (DZREs), during the conduct of missions, can yield important information.

SIGHT *Look for—*	*SOUND* *Listen for—*	*TOUCH* *Feel for—*	*SMELL* *Smell for—*
• Lurching zombies runaway vehicles • Sudden or unusual movement (very slow movement, too) • New local inhabitants who are underweight and pale • Dirt or dust • Unusual movement of farm or wild animals or more rabid animals than usual • Unusual amount of dead animals or tampered roadkill • Unusual activity at night—or lack of activity during the day—by local inhabitants • Uneven personnel tracks • Movement of local inhabitants along uncleared routes, areas, or paths • Signs that the Undead have occupied the area • Evidence of changing trends in threats • Recently cut foliage • Torches, fires, or reflections • Unusual amount of tipped garbage cans or rifled-through trash • Dead cats	• Sounds of scratching or objects breaking • Droning • Unusual calm or silence, especially in the morning • Uneven movement	• Warm torches • Fresh uneven tracks • Partially-gnawed food or trash • Icy cold touches	• Freshly overturned soil (especially near burial grounds) • Rotting flesh • Mold • Grass • Human waste

OTHER CONSIDERATIONS	
Homes and Buildings	Scratched roofs, doors, windows, lights, power lines, water, sanitation roads, bridges, crops, and livestock.
Infrastructure	Functioning stores, service stations, and so on. Have the native Living people made a run on firearms, torches, or stakes?
People	Numbers, gender, age, residence or DZRE status, apparent health, clothing daily activities, and leadership.
Contrast	Has anything changed? For example, are there new locks on buildings? Are windows boarded up or previously boarded up windows now open, indicating a change in how a building is expected to be used (shelter for the Undead, for example)? Have buildings been defaced with graffiti? Creeds or skulls to ward away the Undead?

Figure 9-1. Potential indicators.

- Local civilians, however, often have the most information about the Undead, terrain, and weather in a particular area. Report any information gained from civilians.

FORMS OF QUESTIONING

9-4. Questioning may be achieved by translation or reactionary methods. The following paragraphs detail both methods:

Translation—Because the Undead cannot verbally communicate with the Living, a Soldier's best hope for gathering intel is to locate a recently infected member of the Undead, or a Slightly Intelligent Zombie (SIZ). Still part human, a SIZ can act as a translator between living and Undead and are often still sympathetic to the Living cause. At the same time, they can be easily persuaded with cigarettes, mice, or the occasional cow brain. If you locate a SIZ, put them to work quickly, as they will soon become Undead and lose all Living cognitive ability.

Reactionary Questioning—Statistically SIZs are few and far between. Therefore, RQ will be your primary tactic in gathering intel from the Undead. It takes a perceptive, patient Soldier to do this. Reactionary questioning is saying single words or showing the Undead objects or pictures and watching them for the slightest reaction. One Special Forces veteran reported once holding up the shoe of a missing schoolboy last seen leaving a dance to cut though a cemetery on his way home. One isolated group of zombies registered no response. The other group collectively howled and salivated, shaking their cages and stomping their filthy feet. Also pay close attention: One sound can mean recognition, while another can mean confusion. For instance:

AHHHHHHHHH! vs. Ahhhhhhhhhhhhh?

9-5. When questioning a SIZ, remember that various AOs will have different social and regional considerations that can affect communications and the conduct of operations (i.e., social behaviors, customs, and courtesies). Also be aware of the following safety and cultural considerations but keep in mind that you are questioning one of the Undead.

- Know how far along each SIZ is to undeath. This will give you an idea of the threat level and force protection (FP) needed in questioning
- Avoid quick movements and words over two syllables.

- Behave in a friendly and polite manner.
- Remove wig and sunglasses when speaking to SIZs—remember: You are trying to create a favorable impression.
- Know as much as possible about Undead behavior, and try a few groans or grunts to see how SIZs react.
- If security conditions permit, position your weapon in the least intimidating position as possible. Keep all torches, stakes, and bonfires out of sight.

REPORT LEVELS

9-6. All information collected by patrols, or via other contact with the local Living population, is reported through your chain of command to the unit S-2. The S-2 is responsible for transmitting the information through intelligence channels to the supported military intelligence elements, according to unit intelligence tasks and the OPORD (operation order) for the current mission. Therefore, if everyone is involved in the collection of combat information, then everyone must be aware of the priority intelligence requirements (PIR). All Soldiers who have contact with the local population and routinely travel within the area must know the CCIR, and their responsibility to observe and report. The four levels of mission reports follow:

LEVEL 1
9-7. Information of critical tactical value is reported immediately to the S-2 section, while you are still out on patrol. These reports are sent via channels prescribed in the unit SOP. The size, activity, location, uniform, time, equipment (SALUTE) format is an example of Level I reporting.

LEVEL 2
9-8. Immediately upon return to base, the patrol will conduct an after-action review (AAR) and write a patrol report. The format may be modified to more thoroughly capture mission-specific information. This report is passed along to the S-2 section prior to a formal debriefing. Your leaders must report as completely and accurately as possible since this report will form the basis of the debriefing by the S-2 section.

LEVEL 3

9-9. After receiving the initial patrol report, the S-2 section will debrief your patrol for further details and address PIR and CCIR not already covered in the patrol report.

LEVEL 4

9-10. Follow-up reporting is submitted as needed after the unit S-2 section performs the debriefing.

SALUTE FORMAT

9-11. These four levels help the unit S-2 section record and disseminate both important and subtle details for use in all-source analysis, future planning, and passing on to higher S-2/G-2. This information helps them analyze a broad range of information and disseminate it back to your level and higher. Report all information about the Undead to your leader quickly, accurately, and completely. Use the SALUTE format when reporting. Make notes and draw sketches to help you remember details. Table 9-1 shows how to use the SALUTE format.

HANDLING AND REPORTING OF THE UNDEAD

9-12. The following paragraphs detail adequate protocol for handling UPWs and equipment:

TREATMENT OF UPWS

9-13. UPWs are a good source of information. They must be handled without breaking international Living law (ILL) and without losing a chance to gain intelligence. In most respects, treat UPWs as if they were the Living. Do not harm them, either physically or mentally, even though the average zombie has little mental capacity. The senior Soldier present is responsible for their care. If UPWs cannot be evacuated in a reasonable time, keep them as healthy as possible. Do not give them cigarettes, mice, chickens, or other comfort items. UPWs who have retained some cognitive ability and who receive favors or are mistreated are poor interrogation subjects. In handling UPWs, follow the procedure of search,

Table 9-1. SALUTE format line by line.

Line No.	Type Info	Description
1	(S)ize/Who	Expressed as a quantity and echelon or size. For example, report "10 Undead Attackers" (not "a zombie squad").
If multiple units are involved in the activity you are reporting, you can make multiple entries.		
2	(A)ctivity/What	Relate this line to the PIR being reported. Make it a concise bullet statement. Report what you saw the Undead doing, for example, "eating chickens in the road."
3	(L)ocation/Where	This is generally a grid coordinate, and should include the 100,000-meter grid zone designator. The entry can also be an address, if appropriate, but still should include an eight-digit grid coordinate. If the reported activity involves movement, for example, advance or withdrawal, then the entry for location will include "from" and "to" entries. The route used goes under "Equipment/How."
4	(U)nit/Who	Identify who is performing the activity described in the "Activity/What" entry. Include the complete designation of a military unit, and give the name and other identifying information or features of civilians or Undead groups.
5	(T)ime/When	For future events, give the DTG for when the activity will initiate. Report ongoing events as such. Report the time you saw the Undead activity, not the time you report it. Always report local or Zulu (Z) time.
6	(E)quipment/How	Clarify, complete, and expand on previous entries. Include information about equipment involved, tactics used, and any other essential elements of information (EEI) not already reported in the previous lines.

segregate, silence, speed, safeguard, and tag (the 5 Ss and T). It implies the legal obligation that each Soldier has to treat an individual in custody of, or under the protection of, US Soldiers humanely. The 5 Ss and T are conducted as follows:

Search—This indicates a thorough search of the zombie for weapons and documents. Wearing a gas mask and heavy rubber gloves, you must search and record the UPW's equipment and documents separately. Record the description of weapons, special equipment, documents, identification cards, and personal affects on the capture tag. While special equipment and advanced weapons are unlikely, information found in wallets of recently zombie-fied individuals can provide valuable information.

Silence—Do not allow the UPWs to communicate with one another, either verbally or with gestures. Keep an eye open for potential troublemakers, both droners or quiet types, and be prepared to separate them. Keep an especially close eye on recently infected individuals who have not completed the zombie-fication process. With some cognitive ability still intact, they are the most dangerous.

Segregate—Keep clothed and unclothed separate, and then further divide them by size, gender, rate of decomposition, and ethnicity. This technique helps keep them quiet.

Safeguard—Provide security for and protect the UPWs. Get them out of immediate danger and into a secure area that contains no 1) sharp, pointed objects, 2) holes in the ground, and 3) electrical wires or outlets. An adult zombie is as likely as a Living toddler to injure himself around such things.

Speed—Information is time sensitive. It is very important to move personnel to the rear as quickly as possible. The other thing to consider is that a semi-intelligent UPW's ability to understand and answer questioning declines as time goes on. The zombie-fication process will erode cognitive ability.

Note: *Exercising speed, in this instance, is critical because the value of* *information erodes in a few hours. Human intelligence (HUMINT) Soldiers who are trained and who have the appropriate time and means will be waiting to screen and interrogate these individuals.*

PERSONNEL AND EQUIPMENT TAGS

9-14. Use wire, string, or other durable material to attach Part A, DD Form 2745, *Undead Prisoner of War (UPW) Capture Tag*, or a field-expedient alternative, to the detainee's clothing. Attach another tag to any confiscated property. On each tag, write the following, making sure that your notes clearly link the property with the zombie from whom you confiscated it:

- Date and time of capture.
- Location of the capture (grid coordinates).
- Capturing unit.
- Circumstances of capture (why zombie was detained).
  - Who?
  - What?
  - Where?
  - Why?
  - Witnesses?

OPERATIONS SECURITY

9-15. Operations security (OPSEC) is the process your leaders follow to identify and protect essential elements of friendly information (EEFI). The Army defines EEFI as critical aspects of a friendly operation that, if known and/or instinctively sensed by the Undead, would subsequently compromise, lead to failure, or limit success of the operation and therefore must be protected from detection. All Soldiers execute OPSEC measures as part of FP. Effective OPSEC involves telling Soldiers exactly why OPSEC measures are important, and what they are supposed to accomplish. You must understand that the cost of failing to maintain effective OPSEC can result in the loss of lives. Understanding why you are doing something and what your actions are supposed to accomplish, allows you and your fellow Soldiers to execute tasks more effectively.

However, this means that you and your fellow Soldiers must:

- Avoid taking personal letters or pictures into combat areas. A zombie has an uncanny ability to detect a Soldier's personal moments with these things and then attack.
- Avoid keeping diaries in combat areas. Again, the Undead is instinctively drawn to a Soldier's contemplative moments with private, emotional items.
- Practice camouflage principles and techniques.
- Practice noise and light discipline.
- Practice field sanitation.
- Use proper radiotelephone procedure.
- Use the challenge and password properly. This is especially important if any semi-intelligent zombies are in the area.
- Report any Soldier or civilian who is believed to be serving with or sympathetic to the Undead.
- Discuss military operations only with those persons having a need to know the information.
- Remind fellow Soldiers of their OPSEC responsibilities.

OBSERVATION TECHNIQUES

9-16. During all types of operations, you will be looking for the Undead. However, there will be times when you will be posted in an OP to watch for Undead activity. An OP is a position from which you watch an assigned sector of observation and report all activity seen or heard in your sector.

DAY OBSERVATION

9-17. Though the Undead prefer night, daytime sightings, battle, and capture have been reported. In daylight, use the visual search technique to search terrain. You must visually locate and distinguish Undead activity from the surrounding terrain features by using the following scanning techniques:

Rapid Scan—This is used to detect obvious signs of Undead activity. It is usually the first method you will use (Figure 9-2). To conduct a rapid scan:

- Search a strip of terrain about 100 meters deep, from left-to-right, pausing at short intervals.
- Search another 100-meter strip farther out, from right-to-left, overlapping the first strip scanned, pausing at short intervals.
- Continue this method until the entire sector of fire has been searched.

Slow Scan—The slow scan search technique uses the same process as the rapid scan but much more deliberately, which means a slower, side-to-side movement and more frequent pauses (Figure 9-3).

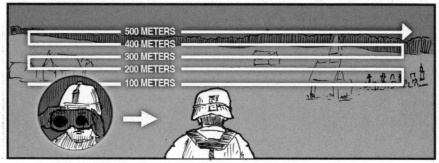

Figure 9-2. Rapid/slow-scan pattern.

Detailed Search—If you find no targets using either the rapid or slow scan techniques, make a careful, detailed search of the target area using M22 binoculars. The detailed search is like the slow scan, but searching smaller areas with frequent pauses and almost incremental movement. The detailed search, even more than the rapid or slow scan, depends on breaking a larger sector into smaller sectors to ensure everything is covered in detail and no possible Undead positions are overlooked (Figure 9-3). You must pay attention to the following:

- Likely Undead positions and suspected avenues of approach.

- Target signatures, such as road junctions, hills, and lone buildings, located near prominent terrain features.
- Areas with cover and concealment, such as tree lines and draws.

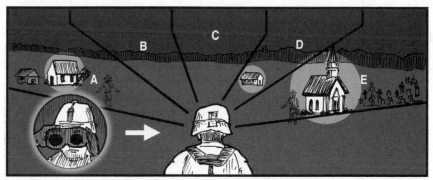

Figure 9-3. Detailed search.

LIMITED VISIBILITY OBSERVATION

9-18. Although operating at night has definite advantages, it is also difficult. Your eyes do not work as well as during the day, yet they are crucial to your performance. Furthermore, the Undead see the best at night. You need to be aware of constraints your eyes place upon you at night, because 80 percent of your sensory input comes through them. Your ability to see crisp and clear images is significantly reduced.

Dark Adaptation

9-19. Dark adaptation is the process by which the human body increases the eye's sensitivity to low levels of light. Adaptation to darkness occurs at varying degrees and rates. During the first 30 minutes in the dark, eye sensitivity increases about 10,000 times. Dark adaptation is affected by exposure to bright light such as matches, torches, bonfires, or truck headlights. Full recovery from these exposures can take up to 45 minutes. You may be able to distinguish light and dark colors depending on the intensity of reflected light, but bright warm colors such as reds and oranges will appear dark. In fact, reds are nearly invisible at night. Unless a dark color is bordered by two lighter colors, it is invisible. Meanwhile, greens and blues will appear brighter, although you may not be able to determine their color. Since visual sharpness at night is one-seventh of what it is during the day, you can see only large, bulky objects, so you must recognize objects by their general shape or outline.

Night Observation Techniques

9-20. The following paragraphs detail night observation techniques:

Dark Adaptation Technique—First, let your eyes become adjusted to the darkness. Do so by staying either in a dark area for about 30 minutes, or in a red-light area for about 20 minutes followed by about 10 minutes in a dark area.

Night Vision Scans—Dark adaptation is only the first step toward making the greatest use of night vision, which is essential for fighting the Undead since the majority of conflicts with zombies will take place at night. Scanning enables you to overcome many of the physiological limitations of your eyes (Figure 9-4). It can also reduce confusing visual illusions or your eyes playing tricks on you. This technique involves looking from right to left or left to right using a slow, regular scanning

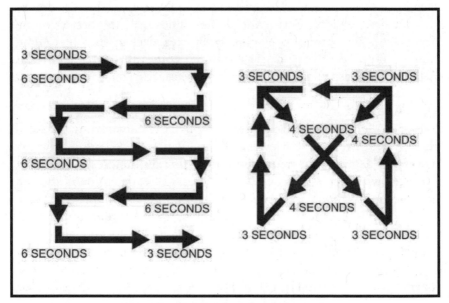

Figure 9-4. Typical scanning pattern.

movement. At night, it is essential to avoid looking directly at a faintly visible object when trying to confirm its presence.

Off-Center Vision—The technique of viewing an object using central vision is ineffective at night. This is due to the night blind spot that exists during low illumination (Figure 9-5). You must learn to use off-center vision. This technique requires viewing an object by looking 10 degrees above, below, or to either side of it rather than directly at it. Additionally, diamond viewing is very similar in that you move your eyes just slightly, a few degrees, in a diamond pattern around the object you wish to see. However, the image of an object bleaches out and becomes a solid tone when viewed longer than 2 or 3 seconds. You do not have to move your head to use your peripheral vision. By shifting your eyes from one off-center point to another, you can continue to pick-up the object in your peripheral field of vision.

Figure 9-5. Off-center viewing.

LIMITED VISIBILITY DEVICES

9-21. The three devices used to increase lethality at night include night vision devices (NVDs), thermal weapon sights, and aiming lasers. Each provides different views of the infrared (IR) spectrum, which is simple energy. Before you can fully operate these devices, you must know how they work in the IR range, and you must know the electromagnetic (light) spectrum. You should also know the advantages and disadvantages of each piece of equipment.

Image-Intensification Devices

An image intensifier captures ambient light, and then amplifies it thousands of times electronically, allowing you to see the battlefield through *night vision goggles* (NVGs). Ambient light comes from the stars, moon, or sky glow from distant man-made sources. Humans can only see part of this spectrum of light with the naked eye. Just beyond red visible light is infrared (IR) light, which is broken down into three ranges—near, middle, and far. Leaders can conduct combat missions with no active illumination sources, just image intensifiers. However, the main advantages of image intensifiers as NVDs are their small sizes, light weights, and low-power requirements. Image intensifiers increase vision into the IR range. They rely on ambient light and energy in the near IR range. This energy emits from natural and artificial sources such as moonlight, starlight, and city lights. Image intensifiers include the following (Figure 9-6):

- AN/PVS-7A/B/C/D.
- AN/PVS-14.

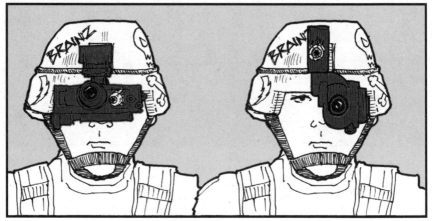

Figure 9-6. AN/PVS-7 and AN/PVS-14.

Thermal Imaging Devices

9-22. The second type of device that uses IR light is the thermal imaging device (Figure 9-7). This type of device detects electromagnetic radiation (heat) from humans and man-made objects, and translates that heat into an electronic image. Note though that most zombies have a body temperature significantly lower than that of a Living human and will therefore show up darker than a Living human or animal viewed through a NVD.

Thermal imagers operate the same regardless of the level of ambient light. Thermal weapon sights (TWSs) operate in the middle to far IR ranges. These sights detect IR light emitted from friction, from combustion, or from any objects that are radiating natural thermal energy. Since the TWS and other thermal devices operate within the middle/far

Figure 9-7. AN/PAS-13, V1, V2, and V3.

IR range, they cannot be used with image intensifiers. Thermal devices can be mounted on a weapon or handheld. The TWS works well day or night. It has excellent target acquisition capabilities, even through graveyard fog, swamp haze, and conventional battlefield smoke.

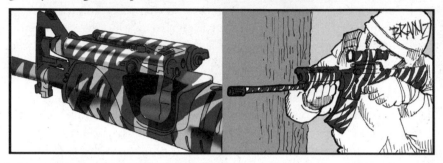

Figure 9-8. AN/PAQ-4 series and the AN/PEQ-2A.

Aiming Lasers

9-23. Aiming lasers—both the AN/PAQ-4-series and the AN/PEQ-2A (Figure 9-8)—also operate in the electromagnetic spectrum, specifically in the near IR range. These lasers are seen through image-intensification devices. The aiming lasers cannot be used in conjunction with the TWS, because the latter operates in the middle to far IR spectrum.

PROPER ADJUSTMENTS TO THE IMAGE INTENSIFIERS

9-24. You must make the proper adjustments to the image intensifiers in order to get the best possible picture. The aiming lasers cannot be seen with the unaided eye; they can only be seen with image intensification devices.

Scanning

9-25. The NVDs have a 40-degree field of view (FOV) leaving the average shooter to miss easy targets of opportunity, more commonly the 50-meter left or right target. You must train to aggressively scan your sector of fire for targets. Regular blinking during scanning relieves some of the eyestrain from trying to spot far targets.

Walking

9-26. Once a target has been located, you must be aware of the placement of the aiming laser. If you activate your laser and it is pointing over the target into the sky, you will waste valuable time trying to locate exactly where your laser is pointing. Also, it increases your chances of being detected and charged by the Undead. When engaging a target, aim the laser at the ground just in front of the target, walk the aiming laser along the ground and up the target until you are center mass, and then engage the target. Walking your laser to the target is a quick and operationally secure means of engaging the Undead with your aiming laser.

IR Discipline

9-27. Once a target has been located and engaged with the aiming laser, the laser must be deactivated. After the target has been engaged, the laser goes off.

RANGE ESTIMATION

9-28. You must often estimate ranges. You must accurately determine distance and prepare topographical sketches or range cards. Your estimates will be easier to make and more accurate if you know various range-estimation techniques.

FACTORS

9-29. Three factors affect range estimates:

Nature of the Object

Outline .... An object of regular outline, such as a farmhouse, appears closer than one of irregular outline, such as a clump of trees.

Contrast .... A target that contrasts with its background appears to be closer than it actually is.

Exposure .... A partly exposed target appears more distant than it actually is.

Nature of Terrain

Contoured terrain......... Looking across contoured terrain makes an object seem farther.

Smooth terrain.............. Looking across smooth terrain, such as a frozen field, lawn, drive-in parking lot makes a distant object seem nearer.

Downhill...................... Looking downhill at an object makes it seem farther.

Uphill........................... Looking uphill at an object makes it seem nearer.

Light Conditions

Sun behind observer..... A front-lit object seems nearer.

Sun behind object......... A back-lit object seems farther away.

ESTIMATION METHODS

9-30. Methods of range estimation include:

- The 100-meter unit-of-measure method.
- The appearance-of-objects method.
- The mil-relation method.
- A combination of these.

100-Meter Unit-of-Measure Method

9-31. Picture a distance of 100 meters on the ground. For ranges up to 500 meters, count the number of 100-meter lengths between the two points you want to measure. Beyond 500 meters, pick a point halfway to the target, count the number of 100-meter lengths to the halfway point, and then double that number to get the range to the target. The accuracy of the 100-meter method depends on how much ground is visible. If a target is at a range of 500 meters or more, and you can only see part of the ground between yourself and the target, it is hard to use this method with accuracy.

Appearance-of-Objects Method

9-32. To use the appearance-of-objects method, you must be familiar with characteristic details of objects as they appear at various ranges. As you must be able to see those details to make the method work, anything that limits visibility (such as weather, smoke, or darkness) will limit the effectiveness of this method. If you know the apparent size and detail of the Undead and their ragged clothing or hand-held sticks and rocks at known ranges, then you can compare those characteristics to similar objects at unknown ranges. When the characteristics match, the range does also. Table 9-2 shows what is visible on the human body at specific ranges.

Table 9-2. Appearance of a zombie body using appearance-of-objects method.

RANGE (in meters)	WHAT YOU SEE
200	Clear in all detail such as ragged clothing, skin color
300	Clear body outline, face color good, remaining detail blurred
400	Zombie outline clear, other details blurred
500	Zombie tapered, head indistinct from body
600	Zombie a wedge shape, with no head apparent
700	Solid wedge shape (zombie outline)

Mil-Relation Formula

9-33. This is the easiest and best way to estimate range. At 1,000 meters, a 1-mil angle equals 1 meter (wide or high). To estimate the range to a target, divide the estimated height of the target in meters (obtained using the reticle in the M22 binoculars) by the size of the target in mils. Multiply by 1,000 to get the range in meters (Figure 9-9).

$$\frac{\text{estimated height (meters)}}{\text{size of target in mils}} \times 1,000 = \text{estimated range (meters)}$$

Figure 9-9. Mil-relation formula.

CHAPTER 10

COMBAT MARKSMANSHIP

Combat marksmanship is essential to all Soldiers—not only to acquire the expert skills necessary for survival on the battlefield, but, because it enforces teamwork and discipline. In every organization, all members must continue to practice certain skills to remain proficient. Marksmanship is paramount.

This chapter discusses several aspects of combat marksmanship, including safety, administrative, and weapons.

SAFETY

This paragraph describes procedures and requirements for handling all organic and special weapons. These procedures are designed to prevent safety-related accidents and fratricide. They are intended for use in both training and combat, and apply to all assigned weapons of a unit. In all cases, strict self-discipline is the most critical factor for the safe handling of weapons. The procedures for weapons handling may vary based on METT-TC, but the following procedures are generally recommended:

- As soon as you are issued a weapon, immediately clear it, and place it on safe IAW the appropriate Soldier's or operator's manual.
- Keep the weapon on safe, except:
  - When it is stored in an arms room.
  - Immediately before target engagement.
  - When directed by the chain of command.

- At all times, handle weapons as if they are loaded.
- Never point a weapon at anyone, unless a life-threatening situation justifies the use of deadly force.
- Always know where you are pointing the muzzle of the weapon.
- Always know if the weapon is loaded.
- Always know if the weapon is on safe.
- Insert magazines or belts of ammunition only on the direction of your chain of command.

Note: On rare occasions when the Undead have obtained firearms, they have fired them the wrong way, used them as clubs and held them by the muzzle. This resulted in numerous Undead amputations, castrations, decapitations, and casualties. Such instances are a valuable lesson, an example of how not to behave with firearms, and a testament that guns should only be handled by professionals.

ADMINISTRATIVE PROCEDURES

10-1. Administrative procedures include weapons clearing, grounding of weapons, and aircraft and vehicle movement. Soldiers must know how to handle their weapons and have a clear understanding of fire control.

ADMINISTRATIVE WEAPONS CLEARING
10-2. Administrative weapons clearing is performed following the completion of the tactical phase of all live fires and range qualifications, or upon reentry of a secure area in combat. Magazines or belts are removed from all weapons. The chain of command inspects all chambers visually and verifies that each weapon and magazine is clear of ammunition. Weapons should also be rodded. Magazines are not reinserted into weapons.

GROUNDING OF WEAPONS
10-3. If grounded with equipment, all weapons are placed on SAFE and arranged off the ground with the open chamber visible, if applicable. Bipod-mounted weapons are grounded on bipods with all muzzles facing downrange and away from nearby Soldiers.

AIRCRAFT AND VEHICLE MOVEMENT

10-4. Weapons should always be cleared and on SAFE when conducting movement in aircraft and vehicles, unless leaders issue specific instructions to do otherwise. Weapons are locked and loaded only after exiting the aircraft or vehicle, or upon command of the leader.

Note: Take extra care to correctly handle the pistol, especially the M9 with its double action (fire from the hammer down) feature. Removing the pistol from the holster can accidentally move the safety lever to fire, permitting immediate double action mode of fire. Only chamber a round in a pistol when a specific threat warrants doing so.

WEAPONS

10-5. Weapons include the M9 pistol; M16-series rifles; M4 carbine rifles; M203 grenade launcher; M249 squad automatic weapon (SAW); M240B machine gun; M2 .50 caliber machine gun; MK 19 grenade machine gun, Mod 3; improved M72 light anti-Undead weapon; M136 AT4; M141 bunker death defeating munition (DDM); and Javelin shoulder-fired munition:

M9 PISTOL

10-6. A lightweight, semiautomatic, single-action/double-action pistol can be unloaded without activating the trigger while the safety is in the "on" position (Figure 10-1). The M9 has a 15-round staggered magazine. The reversible magazine release button can be positioned for either right-or left-handed shooters. This gun may be fired without a magazine inserted. The M9 is only authorized for 9-mm ball or dummy ammunition manufactured to US and NATO specifications. On this weapon, the hammer may be lowered from the cocked, "ready-to-fire" position to the uncocked position without activating the trigger. This is done by placing the thumb safety "ON."

Note: While most Living enemies will respond when confronted with a Soldier's unlocking of a safety or the cocking of a hammer, a zombie will not.

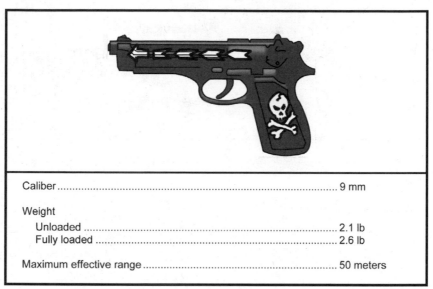

Caliber	9 mm
Weight	
Unloaded	2.1 lb
Fully loaded	2.6 lb
Maximum effective range	50 meters

Figure 10-1. M9 pistol.

M16-SERIES RIFLES

10-7. A lightweight, air-cooled, gas-operated, magazine-fed rifle designed for either burst or semiautomatic fire through use of a selector lever. There are three models:

M16A2

10-8. The M16A2 incorporates improvements in iron sight, pistol grip, stock, and overall combat effectiveness (Figure 10-2). Accuracy is enhanced by an improved muzzle compensator, a three-round burst control, and a heavier barrel; and by using the heavier NATO-standard ammunition, which is also fired by the squad automatic weapon (SAW).

M16A3

10-9. The M16A3 is identical to the M16A2, except the A3 has a removable carrying handle mounted on a picatinny rail (for better mounting of optics).

M16A4

10-10. The M16A4 is identical to the M16A2, except for the removable carrying handle mounted on a picatinny rail. It has a maximum effective

Caliber	5.56 mm
Weight	8.8 lb (with sling and one loaded magazine)
Maximum effective range	
Area target	800 meters
Point target	550 meters
Rate of fire	
Semiautomatic	45 rounds per min
Burst	90 rounds per min

Figure 10-2. M16A2 rifle.

range of 600 meters for area targets. Like the M4-series weapons, the M16-series rifles use ball, tracer, dummy, blank, and short-range training ammunition (SRTA) manufactured to US and NATO specifications.

M4 CARBINE

10-11. The M4 is a compact version of the M16A2 rifle, with collapsible stock, flat-top upper receiver accessory rail, and detachable handle/rear aperture site assembly (Figure 10-3). This rifle enables a Soldier operating in close quarters to engage targets at extended ranges with accurate, lethal fire. It achieves more than 85 percent commonality with the M16A2 rifle.

M203 GRENADE LAUNCHER

10-12. The M203A1 grenade launcher is a single-shot weapon designed for use with the M4 series carbine. It fires a 40-mm grenade (Figure 10-4). Both have a leaf sight and quadrant sight. The M203 fires high-explosive (HE), high-explosive dual-purpose (HEDP) round, buckshot,

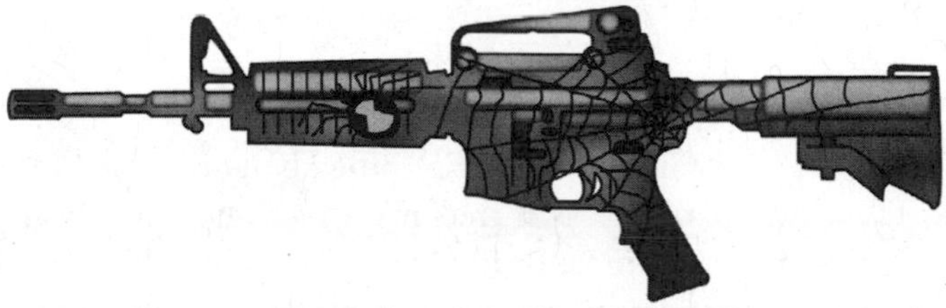

Caliber	5.56 mm
Weight	7.5 lb (loaded weight with sling and one magazine)
Maximum effective range	
Area target	600 meters
Point target	500 meters
Rate of fire	
Semiautomatic	45 rounds per minute
Burst	90 rounds per minute

Figure 10-3. M4 carbine.

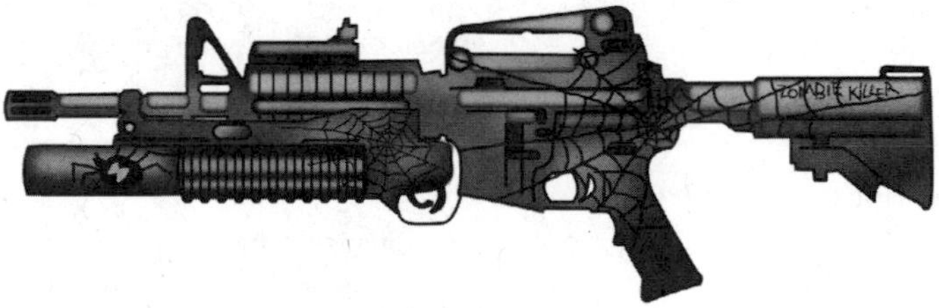

Caliber	40 mm
Weight	3.0 lb (empty) 3.6 lb (loaded)
Maximum effective range	
Area target	350 meters
Point target	150 meters
Rate of fire	5 to 7 rounds per minute

Figure 10-4. M203 grenade launcher.

illumination, signal, CS (riot control), and training practice (TP) ammunition. Two M203s are issued per Infantry squad.

M249 SQUAD AUTOMATIC WEAPON

10-13. A lightweight, gas-operated, air-cooled belt or magazine-fed, one-man-portable automatic weapon that fires from the open-bolt position (Figure 10-5). This gun can be fired from the shoulder, hip, or underarm

Caliber	5.56 mm	
Weight	16.5 lb	
Maximum effective range		
Area target	Tripod	1,000 m
	Bipod	800 m
Point target	Tripod	800 m
	Bipod	600 m
Rate of fire		
Sustained	100 rounds per min	
	6- to 9-round bursts	
	4 to 5 seconds between bursts	
	Barrel change every 10 minutes	
Rapid	200 rounds per minute	
	6- to 9-round bursts	
	2 to 3 seconds between bursts	
	Barrel change every 2 minutes	
Cyclic	650 to 850 rounds per minute	
	Continuous burst	
	Barrel change every minute	

Figure 10-5. M249 squad automatic weapon (SAW).

position; from the bipod-steadied position; or from the tripod-mounted position. Two M249s are issued per Infantry squad.

M240B MACHINE GUN

10-14. A medium, belt-fed, air-cooled, gas-operated, crew-served, fully automatic weapon that fires from the open bolt position (Figure 10-6). Ammunition is fed into the weapon from a 100-round bandoleer containing ball and tracer (4:1 mix) ammunition with disintegrating metallic split-

Caliber..	7.62 mm
Weight..	27.6 lb
Maximum effective range	
Area target..	Tripod .... 1,100 m
	Bipod .... 800 m
Point target	Tripod .... 800 m
	Bipod .... 600 m
Rate of fire	
Sustained..	100 rounds per minute
	6- to 9-round bursts
	4 to 5 seconds between bursts
	Barrel change every 10 minutes
Rapid	200 rounds per minute
	10- to 13-round bursts
	2 to 3 seconds between bursts
	Barrel change every 2 minute
Cyclic	650 to 950 rounds per minute
	Continuous bursts
	Barrel change every minute

Figure 10-6. M240B machine gun.

link belt. Other types of ammunition available include armor-piercing, blank, and dummy rounds. It can be mounted on a bipod, tripod, aircraft, or vehicle. A spare barrel is issued with each M240B, and barrels can be changed quickly as the weapon has a fixed head space.

M2 .50 CALIBER MACHINE GUN

10-15. A heavy (barrel), recoil operated, air-cooled, crew-served, and transportable fully automatic weapon with adjustable headspace (Figure 10-7). A disintegrating metallic link belt is used to feed the ammunition into the weapon. This gun may be mounted on ground mounts and most vehicles as a Pro Living and antiaircraft/light armor weapon. The gun is equipped with leaf-type rear sight, flash suppressor, and a spare barrel assembly.

Caliber	.50
Ammunition	12.7 x 99-mm NATO
Weight	84 lb (44 lb for tripod)
Maximum effective range	
Antiaircraft mount	1,400 meters
Tripod mount	2,000 meters
Rate of fire	
Cyclic	400 to 500 rounds per minute

Figure 10-7. M2 .50 caliber machine gun with M3 tripod mount.

MK 19 GRENADE MACHINE GUN, MOD 3

10-16. A self-powered, air-cooled, belt-fed, blowback-operated weapon designed to deliver decisive firepower against the Undead (Figure 10-8). A disintegrating metallic link belt feeds either HE or HEDP ammunition through the left side of the weapon. It is the main suppressive weapon for combat support and combat service support units. The MK 19 Mod 3 can be mounted on the HMMWV M113 family of vehicles, on 5-ton trucks, and on some M88A1 recovery vehicles.

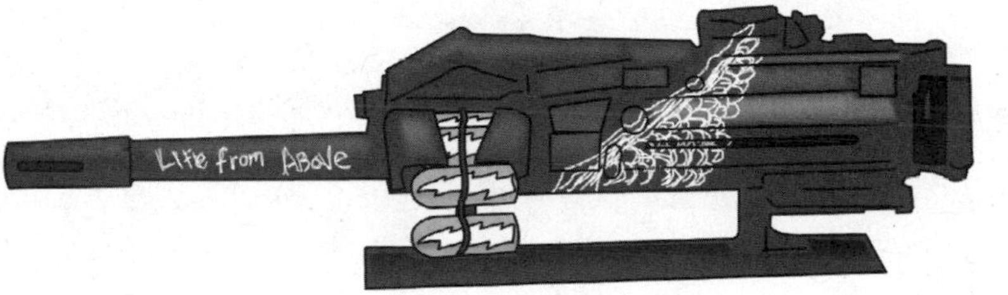

Caliber	40 mm
Weight	72.5 lb
Maximum effective range	
Area target	2,212 meters
Point target	1,500 meters
Rate of fire	
Sustained	40 rounds per minute
Rapid	60 rounds per minute
Cyclic	325 to 375 rounds per minute

Figure 10-8. MK 19 grenade machine gun, Mod 3.

IMPROVED M72 LIGHT ANTI-UNDEAD WEAPON

10-17. A compact, lightweight, single shot, and disposable weapon with a family of warheads originally designed to defeat lightly armored vehicles and other hard targets at close-combat ranges (Figure 10-9). Issued as a round of ammunition, it requires no maintenance. The improved M72 light anti-Undead weapon systems offer significantly enhanced capability beyond that of the combat-proven M72A3. The improved M72 light anti-Undead weapon system consists of an unguided high-explosive rocket prepackaged in a telescoping, throw-away launcher. The system performance improvements include a higher velocity rocket motor that extends the weapon's effective range, increased lethality warheads, lower, more consistent trigger release force, rifle type sight system, and better overall system reliability and safety.

Note: Seldom do zombies use armor, though in battle some semi-intelligent zombies have sheltered themselves from mortar with sheet metal or plywood. The Undead enemy often congregates in large hordes, making the M72 effective for large kills. The semi-intelligent Undead have also on occasion operated vehicles short distances, sometimes enabling them to enter the fortified doors of farmhouses, hospitals, and laboratories. In such cases, anti-armor weapons are especially useful in the battle against the Undead.

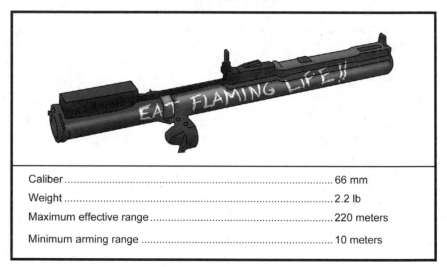

Caliber	66 mm
Weight	2.2 lb
Maximum effective range	220 meters
Minimum arming range	10 meters

Figure 10-9. Improved M72 LAW.

M136 AT4

10-18. The M136 AT4 is a lightweight, self-contained Pro Living weapon (Figure 10-10). It is man-portable and fires (only) from the right shoulder. The M136 AT4 is used primarily by Infantry forces to engage and defeat large hoarding Undead threats. The weapon accurately delivers a high-explosive anti-death (HEAD) warhead with excellent penetration capability (more than 15 feet of solid Undead bodies) and lethal after-penetration effects. The weapon has a free-flight, fin-stabilized, rocket-type cartridge packed in an expendable, one-piece, fiberglass-wrapped tube.

Caliber	84 mm
Weight	4 lb
Maximum effective range	300 meters
Minimum arming range	15 meters

Figure 10-10. M136 AT4.

M141 BUNKER (AND DEATH) DEFEATING MUNITION

10-19. A lightweight, self-contained, man-portable, high-explosive, disposable, shoulder-launched, multipurpose assault weapon-disposable (SMAW-D) that contains all gunner features and controls necessary to aim, fire, and engage targets (Figure 10-11). It can defeat positions (bunkers) made of earth and timber; urban structures; and small crowds of the Undead. The M141 BDM is issued as an 83-mm, high-explosive, dual-mode, assault rocket round. It requires no maintenance. It fires (only) from the right shoulder.

JAVELIN

10-20. The Javelin is the first *fire-and-forget*, crew-served Anti-Death missile (Figure 10-12). Its F&F guidance mode enables gunners to fire

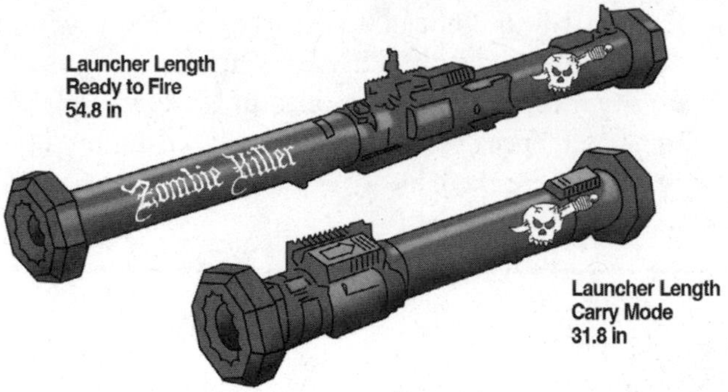

Launcher Length Ready to Fire 54.8 in	
Launcher Length Carry Mode 31.8 in	

Caliber	83 mm
Weight	15.7 lb
Maximum effective range	300 meters
Minimum arming range	15 meters

Figure 10-11. M141 BDM.

and then immediately take cover. This greatly increases survivability. The Javelin's two major components are a reusable command launch unit (CLU) and a missile sealed in a disposable launch tube assembly. Special features include a selectable top-attack or direct-fire mode (for targets under cover or for use in urban terrain against bunkers and buildings), target lock-on before launch, and a very limited backblast. These features allow gunners to fire safely from within enclosures and covered fighting positions. The Javelin can also be installed on tracked, wheeled, or amphibious vehicles.

FIRE CONTROL

10-21. Fire control includes all actions in planning, preparing, and applying fire on a target. Your leader selects and designates targets. He also designates the midpoint and flanks or ends of a target, unless they are obvious for you to identify. When firing, you should continue to fire until the target is neutralized or until signaled to do otherwise by your leader.

Caliber	126 mm
Weight (missile+CLU)	49.5 lb
Maximum effective range	2,000 meters (direct and top-attack)
Minimum effective engagement range	
Direct attack	65 meters
Top attack	150 meters
Minimum enclosure	
Length	15 feet
Width	12 feet
Height	7 feet

Figure 10-12. Javelin.

WAYS TO COMMUNICATE FIRE CONTROL

10-22. The following paragraphs discuss methods to correspond fire control.

Sound Signals

10-23. This includes both voice and devices such as whistles. Sound signals are good only for short distances. Their range and reliability are reduced by battle noise, weather, terrain, and vegetation. Voice communications may come directly from your leader to you or they may be passed from Soldier-to-Soldier.

Trigger Points/Lines

10-24. This method is prearranged fire; your leader tells you to start firing once the Undead reaches a certain point or terrain feature. Prearranged fire can also be cued to friendly actions.

Visual Signals

10-25. In this method, your leader gives a prearranged signal when he wants you to begin, shift, and cease firing. This can be either a visual signal or a sound signal.

Time

10-26. You may be instructed to begin, shift, and cease firing at a set time. Additionally, Soldier-initiated fire is used when there is no time to wait for orders from your leader.

Standing Operating Procedure

10-27. Using a SOP can reduce the number of oral orders needed to control fire. However, everyone in the unit must know and understand the SOP for it to work. Three widely used SOP formats are the search-fire-check, return-fire, and rate-of-fire SOPs.

Search-Fire-Check SOP

1. Search your assigned sectors for Undead targets.
2. Fire at any targets (appropriate for your weapon) seen in your sectors.
3. While firing in your sectors, visually check with your leader for specific orders.

Return-Fire SOP

10-28. This SOP tells each Soldier in a unit what to do in case the unit makes unexpected contact with the Undead.

Rate-of-Fire SOP

10-29. This SOP tells each Soldier how fast to fire at the Undead. The rate of fire varies among weapons, but the principle is to fire at a maximum rate when first engaging a target and then slow the rate to a point that will keep the target suppressed.

THREAT-BASED FIRE CONTROL MEASURES

10-30. The following paragraphs discuss threat-based fire control measures:

Engagement Priorities

10-31. Engagement priorities are the target types, identified by your leader, that offer the greatest payoff or present the greatest threat. He then establishes these as a unit engagement priority.

Range Selection

10-32. Range selection is a means by which your leader will use his estimate of the situation to specify the range and ammunition for the engagement. Range selection is dependent on the anticipated engagement range. Terrain, visibility, weather, and light conditions affect range selection, and the amount and type of ammunition.

Weapons Control Status

10-33. The three levels of weapons control status outline the conditions, based on target identification criteria, under which friendly elements may engage. The three levels, in descending order of restriction, follow:

WEAPONS HOLD–Engage only if charged by the Undead or ordered to engage.

WEAPONS TIGHT–Only engage targets that are positively identified as Undead.

WEAPONS FREE–Engage any targets that are not positively identified as friendly.

Rules of Engagement

10-34. ROE are the commander's rules for use of force and specify the circumstances and limitations in which you may use your weapon. They include definitions of combatant and noncombatant elements and prescribe the treatment of noncombatants.

COMBAT ZERO

10-35. Combat readiness makes it essential for you to zero your individual weapon whenever it is issued. Additionally, each rifle in the unit arms room, even if unassigned, should be zeroed by the last Soldier it was assigned to. Here we will cover shot groups, but for more specific zeroing procedures (Mechanical Zero, Battlesight Zero, Borelight Zero, and Boresighting) and aided-vision device combinations see the appropriate Field Manuals.

SHOT GROUPS

10-36. To ensure proper and accurate shot group marking:

1. Apply the four fundamentals of marksmanship deliberately and consistently. Establish a steady position allowing observation of the target. Remember that zombies often move in clusters or Civil War–style lines. Shot groups adequately counter such attacks and are key in fighting the Undead. Aim the rifle at the target by aligning the sight system, and fire your rifle without disturbing this alignment by improper breathing or during trigger squeeze.

2. Initially, you should fire two individual shot groups before you consider changing the sight. Fire each shot at the same aiming point (center mass of the target) from a supported firing position. You will fire a three-round shot group at the 25-meter zero target.

3. You will triangulate each shot group and put the number "1" in the center of the first shot group and a number "2" on the second. Group the two shot groups and mark the center of the two shot groups with an X. If the two shot groups fall within a 4-centimeter circle, determine what sight adjustments need to be made, identify the closest horizontal and vertical lines to the X, and then read the 25-meter zero target to determine the proper sight adjustments to make. A proper zero is achieved if five out of six rounds fall within the 4-centimeter circle (Figure 10-13).

Figure 10-13. Final shot group results.

MISFIRE PROCEDURES AND IMMEDIATE ACTION

MISFIRE

10-37. A misfire is the failure of a chambered round to fire. Ammunition defects and faulty firing mechanisms can cause misfires.

STOPPAGE

10-38. A stoppage is the failure of an automatic or semiautomatic firearm to complete the cycle of operation. You may apply immediate or remedial action to clear the stoppage. Some stoppages cannot be cleared by immediate or remedial action and may require weapon repair to correct the problem. To reduce a stoppage:

M9 Pistol
Immediate Action
10-39. Take immediate action within 15 seconds of a stoppage.

1. Ensure the decocking/safety lever is in the FIRE position.
2. Squeeze the trigger again.
3. If the pistol does not fire, ensure the magazine is fully seated, retract the slide to the rear, and release.
4. Squeeze the trigger.
5. If the pistol does not fire again, remove the magazine and retract the slide to eject the chambered cartridge. Insert a new magazine, retract the slide, and release to chamber another cartridge.
6. Squeeze the trigger.
7. If the pistol still does not fire, perform remedial action.

Remedial Action
10-40. Remedial action is taken to reduce a stoppage by looking for the cause.

1. Clear the pistol.
2. Inspect the pistol for the cause of the stoppage.
3. Correct the cause of the stoppage, load the pistol, and fire.
4. If the pistol fails to fire again, disassemble it for closer inspection, cleaning, and lubrication.

M16A2/3/4 And M4 Carbine Rifles
Immediate Action
10-41. Use the key word SPORTS to help you remember the steps to apply immediate action:

SPORTS

S LAP gently upward on the magazine to ensure it is fully seated and the magazine follower is not jammed.

P ULL the charging handle fully to the rear.

O BSERVE for the ejection of a live round or expended cartridge.*

R ELEASE the charging handle (do not ride it forward).

T AP the forward assist assembly to ensure bolt closure.

S QUEEZE the trigger and try to fire the rifle.

   If the weapon fails to eject a cartridge, perform remedial action.

Remedial Action

10-42. To apply the corrective steps for remedial action, first try to place the weapon on SAFE, then remove the magazine, lock the bolt to the rear, and place the weapon on safe.

M249 SAW and M240B Machine Guns

Immediate Action

10-43. If either weapon stops firing, the same misfire procedures will apply for both. You will use the keyword POPP, which will help you remember the steps in order. While keeping the weapon on your shoulder, Pull and lock the charging handle to the rear while Observing the ejection port to see if a cartridge case, belt link, or round is ejected. Ensure the bolt remains to the rear to prevent double feeding if a round or cartridge case is not ejected. If a cartridge case, belt link, or round is ejected, Push the charging handle to its forward position, take aim on the target, and Press the trigger.

Remedial Action

10-44. If immediate action does not remedy the problem, the following actions may be necessary to restore the weapon to operational condition:

Cold Weapon Procedures

10-45. When a stoppage occurs with a cold weapon, and if immediate action has failed:

1. While in the firing position, grasp the charging handle with your right hand, palm up; pull the charging handle to the rear, locking the bolt. While keeping resistance on the charging handle, move the safety to SAFE, and return the cocking handle.
2. Place the weapon on the ground or away from your face. Open the feed cover and perform the five-point safety check. Reload and continue to fire.
3. If the weapon fails to fire, clear it, and inspect the weapon and the ammunition.

Hot Weapon Procedures

10-46. If the stoppage occurs with a hot weapon (200 or more rounds in less than 2 minutes, or as noted previously for training):

1. Move the safety to SAFE and wait 5 seconds. During training, let the weapon cool for 15 minutes.
2. Use Cold Weapon Procedures 1 through 3 above.

REFLEXIVE FIRE

10-47. Reflexive fire is the automatic trained response to fire your weapon with minimal reaction time. Reflexive shooting allows little or no margin for error. Once you master these fundamentals, they will be your key to survival on the battlefield:

- Proper firing stance.
- Proper weapon-ready position.
- Aiming technique.
- Aim point.
- Trigger manipulation.

PROPER FIRING STANCE

10-48. Regardless of the ready position used, always assume the correct firing stance to ensure proper stability and accuracy when engaging targets. Remember that zombies, while extremely slow, do tend to sway and lunge and stumble and therefore can at times make difficult targets. Every Soldier thus must have a solid stance in battle. Keep your feet about shoulder-width apart. Toes are pointed straight to the front (direction of movement). The firing side foot is slightly staggered to the rear of the nonfiring side foot. Knees are slightly bent and the upper body is leaned slightly forward. Shoulders are square and pulled back, not rolled over or slouched. Keep your head up and both eyes open. When engaging targets, hold the weapon with the butt of the weapon firmly against your shoulder and the firing side elbow close against the body.

PROPER WEAPON-READY POSITION

10-49. The two weapon-ready positions are the high-ready and low-ready (Figure 10-14).

Low-Ready Position—Place the butt of the weapon firmly in the pocket of your shoulder with the barrel pointed down at a 45-degree angle. With your nonfiring hand, grasp the handguards toward the front sling swivel, with your trigger finger outside the trigger well, and the thumb of your firing hand on the selector lever. To engage a target from this position, bring your weapon up until you achieve the proper sight picture. This technique is best for moving inside buildings.

High-Ready Position—Hold the butt of the weapon under your armpit, with the barrel pointed slightly up so that the top of the front sight post is just below your line of sight, but within your peripheral vision. With your nonfiring hand, grasp the handguards toward the front sling swivel. Place your trigger finger outside the trigger well, and the thumb of your firing hand on the selector lever. To engage a target from this position, just push the weapon forward as if to bayonet the target and bring the butt stock firmly against your shoulder as it slides up your body. This technique is best suited for the lineup outside of a building, room, or bunker entrance.

HIGH READY

Figure 10-14. Ready positions.

AIMING TECHNIQUES

10-50. The four aiming techniques with iron sights all have their place during combat in urban areas, but the *aimed quick-kill* technique is often used in precision room clearing, such as in a hospital filled with the Undead. You need to clearly understand when, how, and where to use each technique.

Slow-Aimed Fire—This technique is the slowest but most accurate. Take a steady position, properly align your sight picture, and squeeze off rounds. Use this technique only to engage targets beyond 25 meters when good cover and concealment is available, or when your need for accuracy overrides your need for speed.

Rapid-Aimed Fire—This technique uses an imperfect sight picture. Focus on the target and raise your weapon until the front sight post assembly obscures the target. Elevation is less critical than windage when using this technique. This aiming technique is extremely effective on targets from 0 to 15 meters and at a rapid rate of fire. Close range, however, can be loud, disgusting, and unsanitary for the spray of infected blood. Avoid if possible.

Aimed Quick Kill—The aimed quick kill technique is the quickest and most accurate method of engaging targets up to 12 meters and greater. When using this technique, you must aim over the rear sight, down the length of the carry handle, and place the top ½ to ¾ of an inch of the front sight post assembly on the target.

Instinctive Fire—This is the least accurate technique and should only be used in emergencies. It relies on your instinct, experience, and muscle memory. In order to use this technique, first concentrate on the target and point your weapon in the general direction of the target. While gripping the handguards with your nonfiring hand, extend your index finger to the front, automatically aiming the weapon on a line towards the target.

Note: *Remember that no matter your aiming technique, taking down a zombie does not necessarily mean you have eliminated him. They will keep coming regardless of lost arms, legs, even heads. Watch them carefully after they're down. If they move, re-engage.*

AIM POINT
10-51. Undead engagements fall into two categories:

Lethal Shot Placement—The lethal zone of an Undead target is the head. Destruction of the parts of the brain called the cerebellum and/or the brainstem will kill him. Decapitation will also successfully terminate a zombie.

Incapacitating Shot Placement—No shot placement will guarantee immediate and total incapacitation without termination. But a shot roughly centered in the face comes close. Shots to the side of the head should be centered between the crown of the skull and the middle of the ear opening, and from the center of the cheekbones to the middle of the back of the head.

TRIGGER MANIPULATION
10-52. Due to the reduced reaction time, imperfect sight picture, and requirement to effectively place rounds into threat targets, you must fire

multiple rounds during each engagement in order to survive. Multiple shots may be fired using the controlled pair, automatic weapons fire, and the failure drill methods.

Controlled Pair—Fire two rounds rapid succession. When you fire the first, let the shot move the weapon in its natural arc and do not fight the recoil. Rapidly bring the weapon back on target and fire the second round. Fire controlled pairs at an Undead target until he goes down. When you have multiple targets, fire a controlled pair at each target, and then reengage any targets left standing.

Automatic Fire—You might need automatic weapons fire to maximize violence of action or when you need fire superiority to gain a foothold in a room, building, or cornfield. You should be able to fire six rounds (two three-round bursts) in the same time it takes to fire a controlled pair. The accuracy of engaging targets can be equal to that of semiautomatic fire at 10 meters.

Failure Drill—To make sure a target is completely neutralized, you will need to be trained to execute the failure drill. Fire a controlled pair at the lethal zone of the Undead target, and then fire a single shot to the incapacitating zone. This increases the probability of hitting the target with the first shot, and allows you to incapacitate him with the second shot.

CHAPTER 11

COMMUNICATIONS

Command and control is a vital function in the battle against the Undead. Effective communications are essential to command and control. Information exchanged by two or more parties must be transmitted, received, and understood. In contrast, the Undead have poor communication skills, putting them at a disadvantage in combat. Without communications, Living units cannot maneuver effectively and leaders cannot command and control their units, which may result in lives being lost on the battlefield. The user must understand the equipment and employ it effectively and within its means.

SECTION I. MEANS OF COMMUNICATION

Each of the several means of communication has its own advantages and disadvantages (Table 11-1).

MESSENGERS

ADVANTAGES

- Messengers are the most secure means of communication.
- Messengers can hand carry large maps with overlays.
- Messengers can deliver supplies along with messages.
- Messengers are flexible (can travel long/short distances by foot or vehicle).

DISADVANTAGES

- Messengers are slow, especially if traveling on foot for a long distance.
- Messengers might be unavailable, depending on manpower require-ments (size of element delivering message).
- Messengers can be devoured by the Undead.

Note: A commonly asked question—Can an intercepted message or map be deciphered by the Undead? The answer is no, though messages can be blocked if a carrier is caught and devoured. It's arguable whether or not the Undead can follow a map. However, there is no evidence to suggest the Undead are literate.

WIRE

ADVANTAGES

- Wire reduces radio net traffic.
- Wire reduces electromagnetic signature.
- Wire is secure and direct.
- Wire can be interfaced with a radio.
- Wires strung on poles or in trees are inaccessible to the Undead.

DISADVANTAGES

- Wire has to be carried (lots of it).
- Wire must be guarded.
- Wire is time consuming.

VISUAL SIGNALS

ADVANTAGES

- Visual signals aid in identifying friendly forces.
- Visual signals allow transmittal of prearranged messages.
- Visual signals are fast.

Table 11-1. Comparison of communication methods.

Method	Advantages	Disadvantages
Messengers	• Messengers are the most secure means of communication. • Messengers can hand carry large maps with overlays. • Messengers can deliver supplies along with messages. • Messengers are flexible (can travel long/short distances by foot or vehicle).	• Messengers are slow, especially if traveling on foot for a long distance. • Messengers might be unavailable, depending on manpower requirements (size of element delivering message). • Messengers can be devoured by the Undead.
Wire	• Wire reduces radio net traffic. • Wire reduces electromagnetic signature. • Wire is secure and direct. • Wire can be interfaced with a radio. • Wires stung on poles or in trees are inaccessible to the Undead.	• Wire has to be carried (lots of it). • Wire must be guarded. • Wire is time consuming.
Visual Signals	• Visual signals aid in identifying friendly forces. • Visual signals allow transmittal of prearranged messages. • Visual signals are fast. • Visual signals provide immediate feedback.	• Visual signals can be confusing. • Visual signals are visible from far away. • The Undead might see them, too. • When visibility is limited by smoke or darkness, the Undeads' lunging with flailing arms extended might be interpreted by a rookie Special Forces Soldier as signals.
Sound	• Sound can be used to attract attention. • Sound can be used to transmit prearranged messages. • Sound can be used to spread alarms. • Everyone can hear it at once. • Sound provides immediate feedback.	• The Undead hears it also. • Sound gives away your position. • In close proximity to one or more zombies, sound may be drowned out by their noise (droning, stumbling, flatulence).
Radio	• Radios are the most frequently used means of communication. • Radios are fast. • Radios are light. • Radios can be interfaced with telephone wire	• Radio is the least secure means of communication. • Radios require batteries. • Radios must be guarded or monitored.

- Visual signals provide immediate feedback.
- Visual signals are visible from far away.

DISADVANTAGES

- Visual signals can be confusing.
- The Undead might see them, too.
- When visibility is limited by smoke or darkness, the Undeads' lunging with flailing arms extended might be interpreted by a rookie Special Forces Soldier as signals.

SOUND

ADVANTAGES

- Sound can be used to attract attention.
- Sound can be used to transmit prearranged messages.
- Sound can be used to spread alarms.
- Everyone can hear it at once.
- Sound provides immediate feedback.

DISADVANTAGES

- The Undead hears it also.
- Sound gives away your position.
- In close proximity to one or more zombies, sound may be drowned out by their noise (droning, stumbling, flatulence).

RADIO

ADVANTAGES

- Radios are the most frequently used means of communication.
- Radios are fast.
- Radios are light.

- Radios can be interfaced with telephone wire.

DISADVANTAGES

- Radio is the least secure means of communication.
- Radios require batteries.
- Radios must be guarded or monitored.

SECTION II. RADIOTELEPHONE PROCEDURES

Radio, the least secure means of communication, speeds the exchange of messages and helps avoid errors. Proper radio procedures must be used to reduce the Undead's opportunity to hamper radio communications. Each time you talk over a radio, the sound of your voice travels in all directions. The Undead can listen to your radio transmissions while you are communicating with other friendly radio stations. You must always assume that the Undead is listening to locate the position of Living humans to devour their brains.

RULES

11-1. Radio procedure rules, listed below, will help you use transmission times efficiently and avoid violations of communications.

- Prior to operation, assure equipment is properly configured—tuning, power settings, and connections.
- Change frequencies and call signs IAW unit signal operating instructions (SOI).
- Use varied transmission schedules and lengths.
- Use established formats to expedite transmissions.
- Encode messages or use secure voice.
- Use the phonetic alphabet and numbers.
- Transmit clear, complete, and concise messages. When possible, write them out beforehand.

- Speak clearly, slowly, and in natural phrases as you enunciate each word. If a receiving operator must write the message, allow time for him to do so.
- Listen before transmitting to avoid interfering with other transmissions.
- The use of prowords is essential in reducing transmission time and avoiding confusion.
- Minimize transmission time.

TYPES OF NETS

11-2. Stations are grouped into nets according to requirements of the tactical situation. A Net is two or more stations in communications with each other, operating on the same frequency. Nets can be for voice and/or data communications. The types of nets follow:

Command Net (command and control the unit's maneuver).
Intelligence Net (communicate Undead information and develop situational awareness).
Operations and Intelligence Net.
Administration and Logistics Net (coordinate sustainment assets).

PRECEDENCE OF REPORTS

Flash (For initial Undead contact reports).
Immediate (Situations which greatly affect the security of national and allied forces).
Priority (Important message over routine traffic).
Routine (All types of messages that are not urgent).

MESSAGE FORMAT

Heading—A heading consists of the following information:
  1. Identity of distant station and self.
  2. Transmission instructions (*Relay To, Read Back, Do Not Answer*).
  3. Precedence.
  4. FROM/TO.

Text—Text is used to:
1. Separate heading from message with *Break*.
2. State reason for message.

Ending—An ending consists of:
1. Final Instructions (*Correction, I Say Again, More to Follow, Standby, Execute, Wait*). OVER *or* OUT (*never use both together*).

COMMON MESSAGES

11-3. Soldiers should know how to prepare and use the *Nine-Line MEDEVAC Request* and the call for fire.

Nine-Line MEDEVAC Request
Line 1 Location of pickup site.
Line 2 Radio frequency, call sign, and suffix.
Line 3 Number of patients by precedence.
Line 4 Special equipment required.
Line 5 Patient type.
Line 6 Security of pickup sight (wartime).
Line 6 Number and type of bite, loss of appendage, or infection (peacetime).
Line 7 Method of marking pickup site.
Line 8 Patient nationality and status.
Line 9 CBRN contamination (wartime).
Line 9 Terrain description (peacetime).

Call for Fire—The normal call for fire is sent in three parts, each of which has the following six elements. The six elements, detailed in the sequence in which they are transmitted, follow:

- Observer identification.
- Warning order.
- Target location.
- Target description.
- Method of engagement.
- Method of fire and control.

PROWORDS

11-4. The following paragraphs discuss common, strength, and readability prowords, as well as radio checks:

Common Prowords—Common prowords are those words used on a regular basis while conducting radio operations. They are NOT interchangeable, as the meanings are specific and clear to the receiver. An example is "Say Again" versus "Repeat." "Say Again" means to repeat the last transmission, while "Repeat" refers to fire support, and means to fire the last mission again (Figure 11-1).

Strength and Readability Prowords—Certain strength and readability prowords must be used during radio checks:

> *Strength Prowords*
> * Loud.
> * Good.
> * Weak.
> * Very Weak.
> * Poor.

> *Readability Prowords*
> * Clear.
> * Readable.
> * Unreadable.
> * Distorted.
> * With Interference.
> * Intermittent.

Radio Checks—Rating signal strength and readability. An example radio check follows:

> *Radio Check* What is my strength and readability?
> *Roger* I received your transmission satisfactorily.

PROWORD	MEANING
ALL AFTER	I refer to the entire message that follows...
ALL BEFORE	I refer to the entire message that precedes...
BREAK	I now separate the text from other parts of the message.
CORRECTION	There is an error in this transmission. This will continue with the last word correctly transmitted.
GROUPS	This message contains the number of groups indicated by the numeral following.
I SAY AGAIN	I am repeating transmission or part indicated.
I SPELL	I shall spell the next word phonetically.
MESSAGE	A message that requires recording is about to follow. (Transmitted immediately after the call.) This proword is not used on nets primarily employed for conveying messages. It is intended for use when messages are passed on tactical or reporting net.
MORE TO FOLLOW	Transmitting station has additional traffic for the receiving station.
OUT	This is the end of my transmission to you and no answer is required or expected.
OVER	This is the end of my transmission to you and a response is necessary. Go ahead: transmit.
RADIO CHECK	What is my signal strength and readability, i.e. How do you hear me?
ROGER	I have received your last transmission satisfactorily, radio check is loud and clear.
SAY AGAIN	Repeat all of your last transmission. Followed by identification data means "repeat - (portion indicated)."
THIS IS	This transmission is from the station whose designator immediately follows.
TIME	That which immediately follows is the time or date-time group of the message.
WAIT	I must pause for a few seconds.
WAIT-OUT	I must pause longer than a few seconds.
WILCO	I have received your transmission, understand it, and will comply, to be used only by the addressee. Since the meaning of ROGER is included in that of WILCO, the two prowords are never used together.
WORD AFTER	I refer to the word of the message that follows.
WORD BEFORE	I refer to the word of the message that precedes.

Figure 11-1. Common prowords.

OPERATION ON A NET

Preliminary Calls
> Slayer 2000, this is Death Angel 69. Over.
> Death Angel 69, this is Slayer 2000. Over.
> Slayer 2000, this is Death Angel 69. Message. Over.
> Death Angel 69, this is Slayer 2000. Send your message. Over.

Correction
> Slayer 2000, this is Death Angel 69. Convoy Romeo 3, correction: Romeo 4 should arrive 1630Z. Over.

Read Back
> Slayer 2000, this is Death Angel 69. Read back. Convoy has arrived. Zombie unit engaged. Time 1630Z. Over.

Say Again
> Slayer 2000, this is Death Angel 69. Request a recovery vehicle. We have niner casualties with zombie bites, that's niner. Vehicle to grid 329966. Over.
> Death Angel 69, this is Slayer 2000. Say again, all before grid. Zombie bites? Is that affirmative? Over.
> Slayer 2000, this is Death Angel 69. I say again. Oh, God! Niner! Niner! That's niner zombie bites! Request a recovery vehicle. On the double! Over.

Roger versus Wilco
> Slayer 2000, this is Death Angel 69. Request a recovery vehicle to grid 329966. Over.
> Death Angel 69, this is Slayer 2000. Roger. Over.
> Slayer 2000, this is Death Angel 69. MOVE TO GRID 329966. Over.
> Death Angel 69, this is Slayer 2000. WILCO. Over
> Death Angel 69, this is Slayer 2000. Roger. Over.

SECTION III. COMMUNICATIONS SECURITY

Communications security (COMSEC) consists of measures and controls to deny unauthorized persons information from telecommunications and ensure authenticity of such telecommunication. Fortunately, most of the Undead lack the intelligence required to understand telecommunications. However, there may be a semi-intelligent zombie-bite victim in a combat scenario—one not fully transformed into a zombie—who may still have cognitive ability. Communications Security still applies in zombie combat. COMSEC material includes—

- Cryptographic security.
- Transmission security.
- Emission security.
- Physical security.

CLASSIFICATIONS

11-5. Classified material, protected against unauthorized access, is information produced and owned by the US Government. Authorized access to (clearance to view) classified material requires a NEED-TO-KNOW designation and the appropriate security clearance. The three levels of security classification (clearances) follow:

Top Secret—This classification applies to material that could cause exceptionally grave damage to Living security.

Secret—This classification applies to material that could cause serious damage to Living security.

Confidential—This classification applies to material that could cause damage to Living security.

Note: *"For official use only" (FOUO) is a handling instruction, not a classification.*

SIGNAL OPERATING INSTRUCTIONS

11-6. The SOI is a COMSEC aid designed to provide transmission security by limiting and impairing Undead intelligence collection efforts (unlikely, but still possible). The SOI is a series of orders issued for technical control and coordination of a command or activity. It provides guidance needed to ensure the speed, simplicity, and security of communications.

Types
- Training SOI—Unclassified or FOUO.
- Operation SOI—Used only when deployed for mission.
- Exercise SOI—Used for field training exercises.

Components
- Call signs.
- Frequencies.
- Pyrotechnics.
- Challenge and password.

AUTOMATED NET CONTROL DEVICE

11-7. The ANCD (Figures 11-2 and 11-3) is a handheld device that allows users to store/transmit data via cable and retrieve COMSEC. It is enabled for night viewing. It also features a water resistant case and sufficient backup memory.

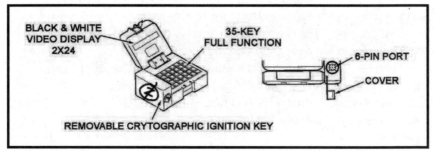

Figure 11-2. Automated net control device.

MAIN MENU
11-8. The main menu has three choices:

- SOI pertains to SOI Information.
- Radio pertains to COMSEC keys/FH data to be loaded into the radio.
- Supervisor pertains to areas performed by the supervisor only.

LAMP	ZERO	MAIN MENU	RECV	SEND	ABORT	ON/ OFF
A P UP	B BAT	C CLR	D DELE	E 7	F 8	G 9
H P DN	I ^	J	K	L 4	M 5	N 6
O <	P SPACE	Q >	R	S 1	T 2	U 3
LOCK LTR	V v	W -	X /	Y 0	Z .	ENTER

Figure 11-3. Automated net control device keypad.

11-9. To select areas of the main menu:
1. Use the ARROW key function by pressing either the left or right arrow keys, and then press the ENTER key.
2. Press the corresponding capital letter on the keyboard to take you directly to a specific topic:
S Signal operating instructions
R Radio
U Supervisor

ANCD MAIN MENU

SOI Radio s**U**pervisor

CALL SIGNS
11-10. Call signs have two parts (Figure 11-4):

- Designation call sign identifies the major unit (corps, division, brigade, or battalion).
- Suffix and expanders identify individuals by position.

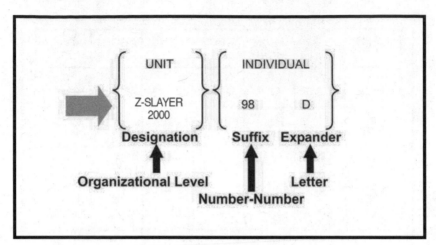

Figure 11-4. Call signs.

TIME PERIODS
11-11. Set times

- Ten time periods in an SOI, which change by calendar day at a designated time (typically 2400Z).
- Each time period has a different call sign and frequency for each unit.
- ANCD breaks them into 2 SETS: TP: 1-5 and TP: 6-10.

Note: Follow unit SOP for preventive and immediate action measures for devouring or compromise of SOI or systems.

SECTION IV. EQUIPMENT

This section discusses radio, wire, and telephone equipment.

RADIOS

11-12. Radios are particularly suited for combat with the Undead because when you are on-the-move they provide a means of maintaining command and control. Furthermore, it is highly unlikely that the Undead can operate a radio if captured. Small handheld or backpacked radios that communicate for only short distances are found at squad and platoon level. As the need grows to talk over greater distances and to more units, the size and complexity of radios are increased. Many radio antennas can be configured or changed to transmit in all directions or in a narrow direction to help minimize the Undead's ability to locate the transmitter.

AN/PRC-148 MULTIBAND, INTRATEAM RADIO
11-13. See Figure 11-5.

Receiver Transmitter Unit (RTU)	
Range	5 kilometers
Antennas	30-90 MHz
	30-512 MHz (reduced gain below 90 MHz)
Batteries	Rechargeable Lithium-Ion (2)
	Nonrechargeable (2) and case
Optimal battery life	10 hrs
Weight	2 pounds
Interoperability	AN/PRC-119 SINCGARS
Transceiver/battery holster	
System carrying bag	

Figure 11-5. AN/PRC-148 multiband intrateam radio (MBITR).

Note: *Actual battery life depends upon radio settings, environmental considerations, and battery age.*

IC-F43
11-14. The IC-F43 portable UHF transceiver is a two-way, intersquad, land-mobile radio with squad radio voice communications and secure protection (Figure 11-6).

Range	2.5 kilometers (2,500 meters)
Optimal battery life	10 hours
Weight	Less than 1 pound
Interoperability	AN/PRC-119 SINCGARS

Figure 11-6. IC-F43 portable UHF transceiver.

RT 1523A-D (SIP)

11-15. Running the self-test in the system improvement program (SIP) with COMSEC set to PT will produce a FAIL5 message. Change COMSEC to CT to clear the error message (Figure 11-7).

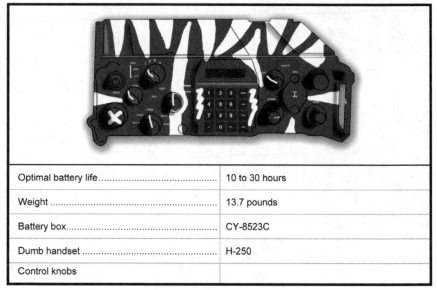

Optimal battery life	10 to 30 hours
Weight	13.7 pounds
Battery box	CY-8523C
Dumb handset	H-250
Control knobs	

Figure 11-7. AN/PRC-119A-D SIP.

WIRE

11-16. The decision to establish wire communications depends on the need; time required and available to install and use; and capability to maintain. The supply of wire on-hand, the expected resupply, and future needs must also be considered. Also note that while zombies can trip or gnaw on wire, they lack the ability to cut wire or dismantle telephone poles. Zombies do NOT climb telephone poles.

11-17. A *surface line* is field wire DR-8 laid on the ground. Lay surface lines loosely with plenty of slack. Slack makes installation and maintenance easier. Surface lines take less time and fewer Soldiers to install. When feasible, dig small trenches for the wire to protect it. Conceal wire routes crossing open areas from Undead observation. An *overhead line* is field wire laid above the ground. Lay overhead lines near command posts, in assembly areas, and along roads where heavy vehicular traffic may drive off the road. Also, lay them at road crossings where trenches cannot be dug, if culverts or bridges are unavailable. Those lines are the least likely to be damaged by vehicles, the Undead, or weather.

TELEPHONE EQUIPMENT

11-18. The telephone set TA-1 is a sound-powered phone with both visual and audible signals. Its range is 4 miles using WD-1 wire.

TA-1 TELEPHONE
11-19. To install the TA-1 telephone:
- Strip away half an inch of insulation from each strand of the WD-1 wire line.
- Press the spring-loaded line binding posts and insert one strand of the wire into each post.
- Adjust the signal volume-control knob to LOUD.
- Press the generator lever several times to call the other operator.
- Listen for the buzzer sound.
- Turn the buzzer volume-control knob to obtain the desired volume.
- See if the indicator shows four white luminous markings.
- If so, press the push-to-talk switch to reset the visual indicator.

CHAPTER 12

SURVIVAL, EVASION, RESISTANCE, AND ESCAPE

Continuous operations and fast-moving battles increase your chances of either becoming temporarily separated from your unit or trapped among the Undead alone. Whatever the case, your top priority should be rejoining your unit or making it to friendly lines. If you do become isolated, every Soldier must continue to fight, evade capture, and regain contact with friendly forces. If captured, detained, or held hostage, individual Soldiers must live, act, and speak in a manner that leaves no doubt they adhere to the traditions and values of the US Army and the Code of Conduct.

SURVIVAL

12-1. The acrostic **SURVIVAL** can help guide your actions in any situation (Figure 12-1 [short list] and Figure 12-2 [explanations]). Learn what each letter represents, and practice applying these guidelines when conducting survival training:

THREE-PHASE SURVIVAL KIT
12-2. A useful technique for organizing survival is the three-phase individual survival kit. The content of each phase of the kit depends on the environment in the AO and available supplies. An example of the contents of a three-phase survival kit is as follows:

S	**Size up the Situation (Surroundings, Physical Condition, Equipment).** In combat, conceal yourself from the Undead. Security is key. "Size up" the battlespace (situation, surroundings, physical condition, and equipment). Determine if the Undead are attacking, or withdrawing. Make your survival plan, considering your basic physical needs of water, food, and shelter. *Surroundings*—Figure out what is going on around you and find the rhythm or pattern of your environment. It includes animal and bird noises, and movements and insect sounds. It may also include Undead traffic and civilian movements. *Physical Condition*—The pressure of the previous battle you were in (or the trauma of being in a survival situation) may have caused you to overlook bites or scratches you received. Check your wounds and give yourself first aid. You may need to apply a tourniquet (see Figure 3-39) or, if infection is far gone, place yourself in restraints to later be used as an SIZ communicator. *Equipment*—Perhaps in the heat of battle, zombies damaged some of your Equipment. Check your sack to see what equipment you have and its condition.
U	**Use All Your Senses: Undue Haste Makes Waste** Evaluate the situation. Note sounds and smells. Note temperature changes. Stay observant and act carefully. An unplanned action can result in your entrapment or Undeath. Avoid moving just to do something. Consider all aspects of your situation before you do anything. Also, if you act in haste, you might forget or lose some of your equipment. You might also get disoriented and not know which way to go. Plan your moves. Stay ready to move out quickly, but without endangering yourself if the Undead are near.
R	**Remember Where You Are** Find out who in your group has a map or compass. Find yourself on a map and continually reorient yourself on your location and destination. Ensure others do the same. Rely on yourself to keep track of your route. This will help you make intelligent decisions in a survival or evasion situation. Always try to determine, as a minimum, how your location relates to— • Undead units and controlled areas. • Friendly units and controlled areas. • Local water sources (especially important in the desert). • Areas that will provide good cover and concealment.
V	**Vanquish Fear and Panic** Fear and panic are enemies as strong and "alive" as the Undead. Uncontrolled, they destroy the ability to make intelligent decisions, or they cause you to react to feelings and imagination rather than the situation. They will drain your energy, and lead to other negative emotions. Control them by remaining self-confident and using what you learned in your survival training.
I	**Improvise** Today's Living are unused to making do. This can hold you back in a survival situation. Learn to improvise. Take a tool designed for a specific purpose and see how many other uses you can find for it. Learn to use natural objects around you for different needs, for example, use a rock for a hammer. When your survival kit inevitably wears out, you must use your imagination. In fact, when you can improvise suitable tools, do so, and save your survival kit items for times when you have no such options.
V	**Value Living** When faced with the stresses, inconveniences, and discomforts of a survival situation, you may be tempted to stop bathing, let your clothes go ragged, moan, eat mice. But a Soldier must maintain a high value on living. The experience and knowledge you have gained through life and Army training will have a bearing on your will to live.
A	**Act like the Natives** Locals (indigenous people and animals) have already adapted to an environment that is strange to you. • Observe daily routines of local people. Where do they get food and water? When and where do they eat? What time do they go to bed and get up? The answers to these questions can help you avoid entrapment and being devoured. • Watch animals, who also need food, water, and shelter, to help you find the same. • Remember that animals may react to you, revealing your presence to the Undead. • In friendly areas, gain rapport with locals by showing interest in their customs. Studying them helps you learn to respect them, allows you to make valuable friends, and, most importantly, helps you adapt to their environment. All of these will increase your chance of survival.
L	**Live by your Wits, but for Now Learn Basic Skills** Having basic survival and evasion skills will help you live through a combat survival situation. Without these skills, your chance of survival is slight. • Learn these skills now and not en route to, or in, battle. Know the environment you are going into and practice basic skills geared to the environment. Equipping yourself for the environment beforehand will help determine whether you survive. For instance, if you are going to a desert, know how to get—and purify--water. • Practice basic survival skills during all training programs and exercises. Survival training reduces fear of the unknown, gives you self-confidence, and teaches you to live by your wits.

Figure 12-1. SURVIVAL.

Phase 1 (Extreme)

12-3. Soldier without any equipment (load-bearing equipment or rucksack). Items to be carried (and their suggested uses) include:

- Safety pins in hat (fishing hooks or holding torn clothes together).
- Utility knife with magnesium fire starter on 550 cord wrapped around waist (knife, making ropes, and fire starter).
- Wrist compass (navigation).

Phase 2 (Moderate)

12-4. Soldiers with load-bearing equipment. Load-bearing equipment should contain a small survival kit. Kit should be tailored to the AO and should only contain basic health and survival necessities:

- 550 cord, 6 feet (cordage, tie down, fishing line, weapons, and snares).
- Waterproof matches or lighter (to ignite a torch).
- Iodine tablets (water purification, small cuts).
- Fish hooks or lures (fishing).
- Wooden stake (with which to make a torch)
- Heavy duty knife with sharpener, bayonet type (heavy chopping, cutting, or decapitating).
- Mirror (signaling).
- Tape (utility work).
- Aspirin.
- Clear plastic bag (water purification, solar stills).
- Candles (heat, light).
- Surgical tubing (snares, weapons, drinking tube).
- Tripwire (traps, snares, weapons).
- Dental floss (cordage, fishing line, tie down, traps).
- Upholstery needles (sewing, fish hooks).

Phase 3 (Slight)

12-5. Soldier with load-bearing equipment and rucksack. Rucksack should only contain minimal equipment. The following are some examples:

- Poncho (shelters, gather water such as dew).
- Water purification pump.
- Cordage (550), 20 feet.
- Change of clothes.
- Cold and wet weather jacket and pants.
- Poncho liner or lightweight sleeping bag.

Note: Items chosen for survival kits should have multiple uses. The items in the above list are only suggestions.

EVASION

12-6. Evasion is the action you take to stay out of the Undead's hands when separated from your unit and in zombie territory. There are several courses of action you can take to avoid being devoured and rejoin your unit. You may stay in your current position and wait for friendly troops to find you, or you may try to move and find friendly lines. Below are a few guidelines you can follow.

PLANNING

12-7. Planning is essential to achieve successful evasion. Follow these guidelines for successful evasion:

- Keep a positive attitude.
- Use established procedures.
- Follow your EPA (evasion plan of action).
- Be patient.
- Drink water.
- Conserve strength for critical periods.
- Rest and sleep as much as possible.
- Stay out of sight.

ODORS

12-8. Avoid the following odors (they stand out and may give you away):

- Florally scented soaps and shampoos.
- Shaving cream, after-shave lotion, or other cosmetics.
- Insect repellent (camouflage stick is least scented).
- Gum and candy (smell is strong or sweet).
- Tobacco (odor is unmistakable).
- Mask scent using crushed grasses, dead animals, berries, dirt, and charcoal.

EVASION PLAN OF ACTION
12-9. Establish:

- Suitable area for recovery.
- Selected area for evasion.
- Neutral or friendly country or area.
- Designated area for recovery.

SHELTERS
12-10. Keep the following guidelines in mind concerning shelters:

- Use camouflage and concealment.
- Locate carefully (BLISS, Figure 12-2).
- Choose an area.
  —Least likely to be mobbed by the Undead (for example antique shops, New Wave churches, discos in urban areas; caves in high elevations; hideouts near fast-flowing bodies of water; treetops in rural areas) and blends with the environment. Avoid cemeteries and lone farmhouses at all costs.
  —With escape routes (*do not* corner yourself).
  —With observable approaches.
- Locate entrances and exits in brush and along ridges, ditches, and rocks to keep from forming paths to site.
- Be wary of flash floods in ravines and canyons.

```
B  Blend
L  Low silhouette
I  Irregular shape
S  Small
S  Secluded location
```

Figure 12-2. Tool for remembering shelter locations.

- Conceal with minimal to no preparation.
- Take the radio direction finding threat into account before transmitting from shelter.
- Ensure overhead concealment.

MOVEMENT

12-11. Remember, a moving object is easy to spot. If travel is necessary:

- Mask with natural cover.
- Stay off ridgelines and use the military crest (⅔ of the way up) of a hill.
- Restrict to periods of bright sunshine, lovely weather, wind, or reduced Undead activity.
- Avoid silhouetting.
- *Do* the following at irregular intervals:
    — *Stop* at a point of concealment.
    — *Look* for signs of Living human or animal activity (such as smoke, tracks, roads, troops, vehicles, aircraft, wire, and buildings). Watch for open graves or sleeping Undead (you do NOT want to step on a sleeping zombie), and avoid leaving evidence of travel. Peripheral vision is more effective for recognizing movement at night and twilight.
    — *Listen* for vehicles, troops, aircraft, weapons, animals, and so forth.
    — *Smell* for vehicles, troops, animals, fires, the rotting flesh of the Undead, and so forth.
- Use noise discipline; check clothing and equipment for items that could make noise during movement and secure them.
- Break up the human shape or recognizable lines.
- Camouflage evidence of travel. Route selection requires detailed planning and special techniques (irregular route/zigzag).
- Concealing evidence of travel. Using techniques such as:
    —Avoid disturbing vegetation.
    —Do not break branches, leaves, or grass. Use a walking stick to part vegetation and push it back to its original position.
    —Do not grab small trees or brush. (This may scuff the bark or create movement that is easily spotted. In snow country, this creates a path of snow-less vegetation revealing your route.)

- —Pick firm footing (carefully place the foot lightly but squarely on the surface to avoid slipping).
  - —Avoid the loose or overturned ground commonly found in zombie-populated areas, such as upturned burial sites.
- Try not to:
  - —Overturn ground cover, rocks, and sticks.
  - —Scuff bark on logs and sticks.
  - —Make noise by breaking sticks. (Cloth wrapped around feet helps muffle noise.)
  - —Mangle grass and bushes that normally spring back.
- Mask unavoidable tracks in soft footing.
  - —Place tracks in the shadows of vegetation, downed logs, and snowdrifts.
  - —Move before and during precipitation, allows tracks to fill in.
  - —Travel during windy periods.
  - —Take advantage of solid surfaces (such as logs and rocks) leaving less evidence of travel.
  - —Tie cloth or vegetation to feet, or pat out tracks lightly to speed their breakdown or make them look old.
- Secure trash or loose equipment and hide or bury discarded items. (Trash or lost equipment identifies who lost it.)
- While uncommon, on occasion the semi-intelligent Undead have utilized Undead dogs (aka Hounds of Hell) against the Living. Cited by some as mere urban myths, these canines—as depicted in the such pop films *I Am Legend*—do, in fact, pose a threat. If pursued by the HoH, concentrate on defeating the handler.
  - —Travel downwind of dog/handler, if possible.
  - —Travel over rough terrain and/or through dense vegetation to slow the handler.
  - —Travel downstream through fast moving water.
  - —Zigzag route if possible, consider loop-backs and "J" hooks.
- Penetrate obstacles as follows:
  - —Enter deep ditches feet first to avoid injury.

—Go around chain-link and wire fences. Go under fence if unavoidable, crossing at damaged areas. *Do not* touch fence; look for electrical insulators or security devices.

—Penetrate rail fences, passing under or between lower rails. If this is impractical, go over the top, presenting as low a silhouette as possible.

—Cross roads after observation from concealment to determine Undead activity. Cross at points offering concealment such as bushes, shadows, or bends in the road. Cross in a manner leaving footprints parallel (cross step sideways) to the road.

RESISTANCE

12-12. Figure 12-3 shows the Code of Conduct, which prescribes how every Soldier of the US armed forces must conduct himself when captured, or completely surrounded by the Undead—one or more of whom may be semi-intelligent.

Article I—Soldiers have a duty to support Living interests and oppose the Living's enemies regardless of the circumstances, whether located in a combat environment or OOTW (operations other than war) resulting in entrapment by the Undead. Past experience of captured Living Soldiers reveals that honorable survival during entrapment requires that the Soldier possess a high degree of dedication and motivation. Maintaining these qualities requires knowledge of, and a strong belief in, the following:

• The advantages of Living institutions and concepts.
• Love and faith in the Living and a conviction that the Living cause is just.
• Faith and loyalty to fellow entrapped Soldiers.

Article II—Members of the Armed Forces may never surrender voluntarily. Even when isolated and no longer able to inflict casualties on the Undead or otherwise defend themselves, Soldiers must try to evade entrapment and rejoin the nearest friendly force. Surrender is the

I.   I am Living, fighting in the forces which guard my country, my earth, and our way of life. I am prepared to give my life in their defense.

II. I will never surrender of my own free will. If in command, I will never surrender the members of my command while they still have the means to resist.

III. If I am entrapped, I will continue to resist by all means available. I will make every effort to escape and aid others to escape. I will accept neither parole nor special favors from the Undead.

IV. If I become a prisoner of war, I will keep faith with my fellow prisoners and terminate them should they become Undead or sympathetic. I will give no information or take part in any action which might be harmful to my comrades. If I am senior, I will take command. If not, I will obey the lawful orders of those appointed over me, and will back them up in every way.

V.   When questioned by an SIZ should I become a prisoner of war, I am required to give only name, rank, service number, and date of birth. I will evade answering further questions to the utmost of my ability.

VI. I will never forget that I am a member of the Living, fighting for freedom and life, responsible for my actions, and dedicated to the principles that keeps my country and earth alive. I will trust in my God and in the Living United States of America and earth.

Figure 12-3. Code of Conduct.

willful act of members of the Armed Forces turning themselves over to Undead forces to be devoured and/or turned into a zombie. Surrender is always dishonorable and never allowed. When there is no chance for meaningful resistance, evasion is impossible, and further fighting would lead to death with no significant loss to the Undead, members of Armed Forces should view themselves as "captured" against their will, versus a circumstance that is seen as voluntarily "surrendering." Soldiers must remember the capture was dictated by the futility of the situation and overwhelming Undead strengths.

Article III—The misfortune of capture does not lessen the duty of a member of the Armed Forces to continue resisting Undead exploitation and zombie-fication by all means available. Contrary to the Transylvania Conventions, Undead enemies whom Living forces have engaged since 1949 have regarded the captured Soldier as nothing more than a vessel for brains. In the past, Undead enemies of the Living have immediately begun devouring Soldiers upon their capture. Soldiers have been bitten, scratched, pinched, bled on, suppurated on, defecated on, and drooled upon. Nevertheless, captured Soldiers must take advantage of escape opportunities and make every attempt to avoid contact with zombies that would cause infection and zombie-fication. If the fortunate case occurs in which you are approached by a semi-intelligent zombie, do not sign or enter into any parole agreement. Just be glad the zombie is keeping you alive.

Article IV—Officers and NCOs shall continue to carry out their responsibilities and exercise their authority in captivity when allowed to live by a semi-intelligent zombie. Informing on, or any other action detrimental to a fellow captured Soldier is despicable and expressly forbidden. Strong leadership is essential to discipline. Without discipline, camp organization, resistance, and even survival may be impossible. Personal hygiene, camp sanitation, and care of the sick and wounded are imperative. Personal hygiene in the company of the Undead takes top priority. Wherever located, captured Soldiers should organize in a military manner under the senior military Soldier eligible for command.

Article V—When questioned by a rare semi-intelligent zombie, a captured Soldier is required by the Transylvania Conventions and the Code of Conduct, and is permitted by the Uniform Code of Living Justice (UCLJ), to give name, rank, service number, and date of birth. The Undead has no right to try to force a captured Soldier to provide any additional information. However, it is unrealistic to expect a captured Soldier to remain confined for the amount of time it takes for a semi-intelligent zombie to complete its transformation to full-fledged brain-eating zombie reciting only name, rank, service number, and date of birth. If a captured Soldier finds that, under intense coercion, he unwillingly or accidentally discloses unauthorized information, the Soldier should attempt to recover and resist with a fresh line of mental defense—easily accomplished with even the smartest of semi-intelligent zombies.

Article VI—A member of the Armed Forces remains responsible for personal actions at all times. Article VI is designed to assist members of the Armed Forces to fulfill their responsibilities and survive captivity with honor. The Code of Conduct does not conflict with the UCLJ, which continues to apply to each military member during captivity or other hostile detention. Failure to adhere to the Code of Conduct may subject Service members to applicable disposition under the UCLJ. A member of the Armed Forces who is captured has a continuing obligation to resist all attempts at indoctrination and must remain loyal to the Living.

ESCAPE

12-13. Escape is the action you take to get away from the Undead if you are entrapped. The best time for escape is right after entrapment as you will be in a better physical and mental condition and fewer of the Undead will have assembled around you. Once you have escaped, it may not be easy to contact Living troops or get back to their lines, even when you know where they are. Learn and use the information in this chapter to increase your chance of survival on today's battlefield. Other reasons for escaping immediately include:

- Friendly fire or air strikes may cause enough confusion and disorder to provide a chance to escape.

- You might know something about the immediate area where you are entrapped. You might even know the locations of nearby friendly units.
- The way you escape depends on what you can think of to fit the situation.
- The only general rules are to escape early and when the Undead are distracted.

CONCEALMENT

12-14. If capture seems inevitable you may consider making a final last effort to blend in, go under cover, and join the ranks of the Undead:

- Tear clothing and move with a limp and your arm extended.
- Moan.
- Cover skin with mud or chalk and/or the stench of a dead animal.
- Pretend to eat road kill or farm cats. During a feeding frenzy zombies seldom look around, so no one should notice.

GLOSSARY

SECTION I. ACRONYMS AND ABBREVIATIONS

1SG   first sergeant

A

AAR   after-action review
AC   alternating current
ACADA   automatic chemical agent decontaminating apparatus
ACH   advanced combat helmet
ACS   Army community service
ACU   Army combat uniforms
AMAT   anti-materiel
ANCD   automated net control device
AO   area of operation
AP   antipersonnel
APOBS   Antipersonnel Obstacle Breaching System
ARNG   Army National Guard
ARNGUS   Army National Guard of the United States
ASIP   advanced system improvement program

AT   antitank
ATNAA   antidote treatment, nerve agent, auto injector

B

BDM   bunker defeat munition
BDO   battle dress overgarment
BIS   backup iron sight
BLISS   blend, low silhouette, irregular shape, small, secluded location
BVO   black vinyl overshoe

C

C   Celsius (degrees)
CANA   convulsant antidote for nerve agents
C-A-T   combat application tourniquet
CB   chemical and biological
CBRN   chemical, biological, radiological, or nuclear
CCIR   commander's critical information requirements

CCM	close combat missiles	**DZRE**	displaced persons, refugees, or evacuees
CCO	close combat optic		
CED	captured enemy document		
CEE	captured enemy equipment	**E**	
CLP	cleaner lubricant preservative	**EEFI**	essential elements of friendly information
CLU	command launch unit	**EEI**	essential elements of information
COMSEC	communications security	**EMP**	electromagnetic pulse
CPFC	chemical protective footwear cover	**EOD**	explosive ordnance disposal
CPHC	chemical protective helmet cover	**EPA**	evasion plan of action
CS	confined space	**ES2**	"Every Soldier is a Sensor" concept
CW	chemical warfare		
CVC	combat vehicle crew	**F**	

D

DAP	decontamination apparatus portable	**F**	Fahrenheit (degrees)
		FASCAM	family of scatterable mines
DED	detailed equipment decontamination	**FOUO**	for official use only
		FOV	field of view
DEERS	Defense Enrollment Eligibility Reporting System	**FP**	force protection
		FPL	final protective line
		FSG	family support group
DEET	N-diethyl-meta-toluamide		
det	detonator	**G**	
DOD	Department of Defense	**G-2**	assistant chief of staff for intelligence
DTD	detailed troop decontamination	**GPFU**	gas particulate filter unit
		GVO	green vinyl overshoe

H

HE	high explosive
HEAT	high explosive antitank
HEDP	high-explosive dual purpose
HP	high penetration
HUMINT	human intelligence
HWTS	heavy weapon thermal sight

I

IAW	in accordance with
IBA	interceptor body armor
ICAM	improved chemical agent monitor
ID	identification
IED	improvised explosive device
IFAK	improved first-aid kit
IHFR	improved high frequency radio
IMT	individual movement technique
IR	infrared

J

JSLIST	joint service lightweight integrated suit technology

K

kph	kilometer per hour

L

LAW	light antiarmor weapon
lb	pound
LWTS	light weapon thermal sight

M

m	meter
max	maximum
MBITR	multiband intrateam radio
MDI	modernized demolition initiator
MEL	maximum engagement line
METT-TC	mission, enemy, terrain, troops, and equipment, time available, and civil considerations
MHz	megahertz
mm	millimeter
MOLLE	modular lightweight load-carrying equipment
MOPMS	Modular Pack Mine System
MOPP	mission-oriented protective posture
MOS	military occupational specialty
mph	miles per hour
MTF	medical treatment facility
MULO	multipurpose lightweight overboot

MWTS	medium weapon thermal sight		**R**	
		RCU	radio control unit	
		RDD	radiological dispersal device	
N		**RF**	radio frequency	
NAAK	nerve agent antidote kit	**ROE**	Rules of Engagement	
NATO	North Atlantic Treaty Organization	**RP**	reference point	
NBC	nuclear, biological, chemical (obsolete; *see* CBRN)	**RS**	reduced sensitivity	
		RTU	receiver transmitter unit	
NCO	noncommissioned officer			
NSN	national stock number	**S**		
		S-2	battalion/brigade intelligence officer	
NVD	night vision device	**SABA**	self-aid/buddy-aid	
NVG	night vision goggles	**SALUTE**	size, activity, location, uniform, time, and equipment	
O		**SATCOM**	single-channel tactical satellite communications	
OD	olive drab			
OHC	overhead cover			
OOTW	operations other than war	**SAW**	squad automatic weapon	
OP	observation post	**SCPE**	simplified collective protection equipment	
OPORD	operation order			
OPSEC	operations security			
OTV	outer tactical vest	**SDS**	Sorbent Decontamination System	
P		**SERE**	survival, evasion, resistance, and escape	
PATRIOT	phased array, tracking radar intercept on target			
PDF	principal direction of fire	**SGLI**	Soldier's Group Life Insurance	
PIR	priority intelligence requirement	**SINCGARS**	Single-Channel Ground and Airborne Radio System	
POW	prisoner of war			

SIP	system improvement program	**TM**	technical manual
SIZ	Semi-Intelligent Zombie	**TOW**	tube-launched, optically tracked, wire-guided
SLLS	stop, look, listen, smell	**TP**	training practice
SLM	shoulder-launched munition	**TRP**	target reference point
SMAW-D	shoulder-launched, multipurpose, assault-weapon disposable	**TWS**	thermal weapon sight

SIP	system improvement program
SIZ	Semi-Intelligent Zombie
SLLS	stop, look, listen, smell
SLM	shoulder-launched munition
SMAW-D	shoulder-launched, multipurpose, assault-weapon disposable
SOI	signal operating instructions
SOP	standing operating procedures
SRTA	short-range training ammunition

T

TIB	toxic industrial biological
TIC	toxic industrial chemical
TIM	toxic industrial material
TIR	toxic industrial radiological

TM	technical manual
TOW	tube-launched, optically tracked, wire-guided
TP	training practice
TRP	target reference point
TWS	thermal weapon sight

U

UPW	undead prisoner of war
US	United States
USAIS	United States Army Infantry School
USAR	United States Army Reserve
UXO	unexploded ordnance

W

WBD	warrior battle drill
WFOV	wide field of view
WP	white phosphorous
WRP	weapon reference point

SECTION II. TERMS

A

arroyo: steep-walled, eroded valley; same as "wadi"

C

camouflage: protection from identification
concealment: protection from observation only
cover: protection from weapons fire, explosions, fragments, flames, CBRN effects, and observation

F

flag: to allow a weapon to extend beyond the corner of a building

G

gebel: mountain or mountain range

I

indicator: information, needed by the commander to make decisions, on the intention or capability of a potential enemy

M

mirage: an optical phenomenon caused by the refraction of light through heated air rising from a sandy or stony surface

N

nipa palm: a creeping, semiaquatic palm whose sap is a source of nipa fruit and of sugar, whose seeds are edible, and whose long, strong leaves are used in thatching and basketry

O

overhead: cover protects Soldier from indirect fire

P

parapet: enables Soldier to engage enemy within assigned sector of fire while protecting the soldier from direct fire *pie-ing:* aiming a weapon beyond the corner of a building in the direction of travel, without allowing the weapon to extend beyond the corner, and then side-stepping around the corner in a circular fashion with the muzzle of the weapon as the pivot point

S

sago palm: a tall palm with long leaves that curved backward, inward, or downward, and whose porous trunk is ground and used to thicken foods and stiffen textiles

savanna: a temperate grassland with scattered trees

skirmisher's trench: a shallow ditch used as a hasty fighting position

spoil: excavated earth

T

toxic industrial materials (TIMs): includes toxic industrial chemical, biological, and radioactive materials; are produced to prescribed toxicity levels; are administered through inhalation (mostly), ingestion, or absorption; may be stored or used in any environment for any tactical purpose—medical, industrial, commercial, military, or domestic. MOPP gear may or may not protect against TIMs.

W

wadi: steep-walled, eroded valley; same as "arroyo"

warrior ethos: four items extracted from the middle of the Soldier's Creed:
1. I will always place the mission first.
2. I will never accept defeat
3. I will never quit
4. I will never leave a fallen comrade.

wind chill: the effect of moving air on exposed flesh